A LITTLE UNION SCOUT

A LITTLE UNION SCOUT

BY

JOEL CHANDLER HARRIS

Illustrated by George Gibbs

The Black Heritage Library Collection

BOOKS FOR LIBRARIES PRESS
FREEPORT, NEW YORK
1972

First Published 1904
Reprinted 1972

Reprinted from a copy in the
Fisk University Library Negro Collection

Library of Congress Cataloging in Publication Data

Harris, Joel Chandler, 1848-1908.
  A little Union scout.

  (The Black heritage library collection)
  Reprint of the 1904 ed.
  I. Title. II. Series.
PZ3.H242Li6 [PS1805]   813'.4   72-2998
ISBN 0-8369-9075-7

PRINTED IN THE UNITED STATES OF AMERICA

LIST OF ILLUSTRATIONS

A LITTLE UNION SCOUT

I

A young lady, just returned from college, was making a still-hunt in the house for old things —old furniture, old china, and old books. She had a craze for the antique, and the older things were the more precious they were in her eyes. Among other things she found an old scrap-book that her mother and I thought was safe under lock and key. She sat in a sunny place and read it page by page, and, when she had finished, her curiosity was aroused. The clippings in the old scrap-book were all about the adventures of a Union scout whose name was said to be Captain Frank Leroy. The newspaper clippings that had been preserved were queerly inconsistent. The Northern and Western papers praised the scout very highly, and some of them said that if there were more such men in the army the cause of the Union would progress more rapidly; whereas the Southern papers, though paying a high tribute to the dash and courage of the scout, were highly abusive. He was "one of Lincoln's hirelings" and as villanous as he was bold.

The girl graduate at once jumped to the conclusion that there was a story behind the old scrap-book, else why should it be preserved by her father, who had been a Confederate soldier? This idea no sooner took shape than she became insistently inquisitive. As for her father, the very sight of the scrap-book awoke the echoes of a hundred experiences—long and dangerous rides in the lonely night, battles, sharp skirmishes and bitter sufferings.

The story, such as it was, took shape in my mind, and I am afraid that the young girl had small difficulty in persuading me to tell it. Memory brought before me the smiling features of Harry Herndon, my life-long friend and comrade, the handsome face of Jack Bledsoe, one of our college mates from Missouri, and the beautiful countenance of his sister, Katherine Bledsoe. These and a hundred other faces came crowding from the past, and the story was told almost before I knew it.

When Harry Herndon and I went to the wars we were somewhat belated. The excitement of '61 found us at college, where we had orders to remain until we had finished the course, and the orders came from one whom we had never dared to disobey—Harry's grandmother. And then, when we were ready to go, she cut in ahead of our plans and sent us to the West with letters to General Dabney Maury, whom she had known when he was a boy and later when he was a young officer in the regular army.

We were not ill-equipped for two raw youngsters ; we had Whistling Jim, the negro, three fine horses, and more money than I had ever seen before. We went to General Maury and were most courteously received. The Virginia Herndons—Harry belonged to the Maryland branch—were related to him—and he liked the name. We caught the barest glimpse of service at Corinth, and were fortunate enough to be in a few skirmishes, where we distinguished ourselves by firing at nothing whatever.

In the course of a few weeks General Maury was made commander of the Department of the Gulf, with headquarters at Mobile, where we saw service as clerks and accountants. For my part, the life suited me passing well, but Harry Herndon fretted so that we were soon transferred to the command of General Forrest, who was sadly in need of men. As it happened, we had little difficulty in finding our man. We had heard that he was in the neighborhood of Chattanooga, giving his men and horses a much-needed rest; but on the way news came to us that, in spite of his brilliant achievements in the field, he had been deprived of the choicest regiments of his brigade —men whom he had trained and seasoned to war. After this mutilation of his command, he had been ordered to Murfreesborough to recruit and organize a new brigade.

Toward Murfreesborough, therefore, we made our way, falling in with a number of Forrest's men who had been on a brief visit to their homes in Alabama and were now returning to their command. As we shortly discovered, the Union commanders in Tennessee mistook General Forrest's movement to the neighborhood of Chattanooga for a retreat; for, shortly after he moved in that direction, an ambitious Federal officer asked and received permission to enter Northern

Alabama with a force large enough to worry the Confederate leader if he could be found. The organization and equipment of this force required a longer time than the Federal commander had counted on, and by the time it was ready to move General Forrest, with the remnant of his command, was on his way to Murfreesborough.

In some way—the sources of his information were as mysterious as his movements—General Forrest learned that a Federal force was making its way toward Northern Alabama, and he did not hesitate to give it his attention. Within a very short time he had followed and overtaken it, passing it on a road that lay parallel to its line of march. Then it was that the Federal commander began to hear rumors and reports all along his route that Forrest was making a rapid retreat before him. It was stated that his men were discontented and that the condition of his horses was something terrible.

One day, along toward evening, the Federal commander went into camp in the neighborhood of a wooded hill that commanded the approach from the south. He felt sure that the next day would witness the rout and capture of the Confederate who had for so long harassed the Federals in Tennessee. As he came to the hill he passed within a few hundred yards of Forrest's men, who were concealed in the woods. The Federals went into camp, while Forrest, leaving a part of his command in the enemy's rear, silently passed around his right flank.

Now, it happened that Harry Herndon and myself, accompanied by Whistling Jim and the companions we had picked up on the way, were coming up from the south. It happened also that we were following the road leading through the valley to the left of the hill on which the opposing forces were stationed. It was very early in the morning, and as we rode along there was not a sound to be heard, save the jingling of our bridles.

The valley had more length than breadth, and was shaped something like a half-moon, the road following the contour of the crescent. We had proceeded not more than a hundred yards along the road within the compass of the valley when a six-pounder broke the silence with a bang, and a shell went hurtling through the valley. It seemed to be so uncomfortably near that I involuntarily ducked my head.

"Marse Cally Shannon," said Whistling Jim, the negro, addressing me, "what you reckon make dem white folks bang aloose at we-all, when we ain't done a blessed thing? When it come ter dat, we ain't ez much ez speaken ter um, an' here dey come, bangin' aloose at us. An' mo' dan dat, ef dat ar bung-shell had 'a' hit somebody, it'd 'a' fetched sump'n mo' dan blood."

Whistling Jim's tone was plaintive, but he seemed no more frightened than Harry was. Following the bang of the gun came the sharp rattle of musketry. We learned afterward that this firing occurred when the advance guard of the Federal commander collided with Forrest's famous escort. We had no idea of the result of the collision, or that there had been a collision. We had paused to make sure of our position and whereabouts. Meanwhile, the little six-pounder was barking away furiously, and presently we heard a strident voice cut the morning air: "Go and tell Freeman to put his battery right in on that gun. I give you five minutes."

"That's our man!" cried one of the troopers

who had fallen in with us on our journey. Joy shone in his face as he urged his horse forward, and we followed right at his heels. In a moment we saw him leap from his horse and throw the bridle-reins to a trooper who was holding a string of horses. We gave ours to Whistling Jim to hold and ran forward with the man we had been following.

We came right upon General Forrest—I knew him from the newspaper portraits, poor as they were. He was standing with his watch in his hand. He looked us over with a coldly critical eye, but gave us no greeting. He replaced the watch in his pocket and waved his hand to a bugler who was standing expectantly by his side. The clear notes rang out, and instantly there ensued a scene that baffles description. There was a rush forward, and Harry and I were carried with it.

I could hear loud commands, and shouting, and the rattle of carbines, muskets, and pistols made my ears numb—but what happened, or when or where, I could no more tell you than the babe at its mother's breast. I could only catch glimpses of the fighting through the smoke, and though I

"He's tryin' to git away!" yelled Forrest in a voice
that could be heard all over the field

I drank in the melody with a new sense of its wild and
melancholy beauty

⌈*Page* 56⌉

was as close to General Forrest as any of his men —right by his side, in fact—I could not tell you precisely what occurred. I could hear cries and curses and the explosion of firearms, but beyond that all was mystery.

I had time during the *mêlée* to take note of the actions of General Forrest, and I observed that a great change had come over him. His face, which was almost as dark as an Indian's when in perfect repose, was now inflamed with passion and almost purple. The veins on his neck stood out as though they were on the point of bursting, and his blazing eyes were bloodshot. Above the din that was going on all around him his voice could be heard by friend and foe alike. I cannot even describe my own feelings.

A courier rode up. He had lost his hat, and there was a spot of blood on his chin. He reported that the Federals were making a desperate effort on the extreme right. "He's tryin' to git away!" yelled Forrest in a voice that could be heard all over the field. "Tell Freeman to take his guns thar and shove 'em in right on top of 'em. We've got the bulge on 'em here, and we're coming right along."

And, sure enough, we began to find less and less resistance in front of us, and presently I could see them running out into the valley, filling the road by which we had come.

II

No pursuit was made at the time, and the Federals, finding that they were not harried, proceeded in a leisurely way toward the river. We followed slowly and at night went into camp, the men and horses getting a good rest. Scouts were coming in to make reports at all hours of the night, so that it was practically true, as one of the old campaigners remarked, that a horse couldn't whicker in the enemy's camp "but what the General 'd hear it sooner or later."

Early the next morning we were on the road, and I had time for reflecting that, after all, war was not a matter of flags and music. The General was very considerate, however—a fact that was due to a letter that General Maury had intrusted to Harry Herndon's care. We were permitted to ride as temporary additions to General Forrest's escort, and he seemed to single us out from among the rest with various little courtesies, which I imagined was something unusual.

13

He was somewhat inquisitive about Whistling Jim, Harry's body-servant, who he thought was a little too free and easy with white men. But he seemed satisfied when Harry told him that the negro's forebears for many generations back had belonged to the Herndons. We halted for a light dinner, and when we had finished General Forrest made a careful inspection of his men as they filed into the road.

We had gone but a few miles when we came to a point where the roads forked. On one he sent a regiment, with Freeman's battery, with instructions to reach the river ahead of the Federals and hold the ford at all hazards until the main body could come up. This done, we swung into the road that had been taken by the Federals and went forward at a somewhat brisker pace.

"I'm going to give your nigger the chance of his life," remarked General Forrest somewhat grimly, "and he'll either fling up his hands and go to the Yankees, or he'll take to the woods."

"He may do one or the other," replied Harry; "but if he does either I'll be very much surprised." General Forrest laughed; he was evidently very sure that a negro would never stand up before gun-fire. A scout came up to report that the Federals were moving much more rapidly than they had moved in the morning.

"I reckon he's got wind of the column on the other road," the General commented. "I allowed he'd hear of it. He's a mighty smart man, and he's got as good men as can be found —Western fellows. If he had known the number of my men in the woods back yander he'd 'a' whipped me out of my boots." And then his eye fell again on Whistling Jim, who was laughing and joking with some of the troopers. He called to the negro in stern tones, and ordered him to ride close to his young master. "We are going to have a little scrimmage purty soon, and a nigger that's any account ought to be right where he can help his master if he gets hurt."

Whistling Jim's face, which had grown very serious when he heard his name called by the stern commander, suddenly cleared up and became illuminated by a broad grin. "You hear dat, Marse Harry!" he exclaimed. "I'm gwine in right behime you!" He reflected a moment, and then uttered an exclamation of "Well, suh!"

About four o'clock in the afternoon the troopers under General Forrest came in contact with Federals. This was in the nature of a surprise to the Union commander, for there were persistent reports that Forrest had passed on the other road, with the evident intention of harrying the Federals at a point where they had no intention of crossing. So well assured was he that these reports were trustworthy that he was seriously considering the advisability of detaching a force sufficiently large to capture the Confederate. He therefore paid small attention to the attacks on his rear-guard. But presently the pressure became so serious that he sent a member of his staff to investigate it.

Before the officer could perform this duty the rear-guard was compelled to retreat on the main body in the most precipitate manner. Then the attack ceased as suddenly as it began, and the Federal commander concluded that, under all the circumstances, it would be best to cross the river and get in touch with his base of supplies.

He went forward as rapidly as his troops could march, and he had a feeling of relief when he came in sight of the river. It was higher than it had been when he crossed it three or four days

before, but still fordable; but as his advance
guard began to cross, Freeman's battery, oper-
ated by young Morton, opened on them from the
ambuscade in which it had been concealed.   The
thing to do, of course, was to charge the battery
and either capture it or silence it, and the Federal
commander gave orders to that effect.   But Forrest, looking at the matter from a diametrically
opposite point of view, knew that the thing to do
was to prevent the capture of the battery, and so
he increased the pressure upon the Federal rear
to such an extent that his opponent had no time
to attend to the Confederate battery.

The Union commander was a very able man
and had established a reputation as a good fighter.
So now, with perfect coolness, he managed to
present a very strong front where the rear had
been, and he made desperate efforts to protect
his flank.   But he was too late.   Forrest said
afterward that it was as pretty a move as he had
ever seen, and that if it had been made five minutes sooner it would probably have saved the day.

Just as the movement was about to be com-
pleted it was rendered useless by the charge of
Forrest's escort, a picked body of men, led by

the General in person. In the circumstances such charges were always irresistible. Before the Federals could recover, the Confederate general, by means of a movement so sudden that no commander could have foreseen it, joined his force with that which was supporting Freeman's battery and charged all along the line, bringing the eight and twelve-pounders right to the front. No men, however brave, could stand before a battery at close range, and the inevitable result ensued—they got out of the way, and stood not on the order of their going. They floundered across the river as best they could, and if they had not been American troops they would have been demoralized and rendered useless for fighting purposes; but, being what they were, they showed their courage on many a hard-fought field as the war went on.

When night fell we retired a mile or two from the river and went into camp. Forrest was in high good-humor. He had accomplished all that he had set out to accomplish, and more. He had emphasized the fact that it was dangerous work for the Federals to raid Northern Alabama while he was in striking distance, and he had captured army stores and secured horses that were comparatively fresh. The most welcome capture was the arms, for many of his men were armed with flintlock muskets.

He was very talkative. "That nigger of yours done about as well as any of the balance of us," he said to Harry Herndon.

"I didn't see him at all during the fighting," replied Harry, "but I told him you'd have him shot if he ran."

"Well, he went right in," remarked the General, "and I expected him to go over to the Yankees. Maybe he'd 'a' gone if it hadn't been for the water."

At that moment we heard Whistling Jim calling, "Marse Harry! Marse Cally Shannon!" I answered him so that he could find us, and he came up puffing and blowing. A red handkerchief was tied under his chin and over his head.

"Marse Harry!" he exclaimed, "kin I see you an' Marse Cally Shannon by yo'se'f? I done done sump'n dat you'll sho kill me 'bout."

"Well, don't make any secret of it," said I. "Out with it!" exclaimed Harry.

"Marse Harry, I done gone an' shot Marse Jack Bledsoe."

"Good Lord!" cried Harry.

"Yasser, I done shot 'im, an' he's bad hurt, too. You know dat las' time we went at um? Well, suh, I wuz shootin' at a man right at me, an' he knock my han' down des ez I pull de trigger, an' de ball cotch him right 'twix de hip an' de knee. He call me by my name, an' den it come over me dat we done got mix' up in de shuffle an' dat I wuz shootin' at you. But 'twuz Marse Jack Bledsoe; I know'd 'im time I look at 'im good."

"Good heavens! Is he dead?" inquired Harry, his voice shaking a little in spite of himself.

"He ain't dead yit, suh," replied Whistling Jim. "I got down off'n my hoss an' pick 'im up an' take 'im out er de paff er de rucus, an' den when you-all done des ez much shootin' an' killin' ez you wanter, I went back an' put 'im on my hoss an' tuck 'im ter dat little house by de river. Dey's a white lady dar, an' she say she'll take keer un' 'im twel somebody come. Does you reckon any er his side gwineter come back atter 'im, Marse Harry? Kaze ef dey don't, I dunner what de name er goodness he gwineter do. Dar he is, an' dar he'll lay.   I'm done sick er war ef you call dis war—you hear me!"

Harry said nothing, but I knew he was thinking of the fair Katherine, Jack's sister, and wondering if he would ever be to her what she was to him.   He had his face in his hands, and appeared ready to give way to grief.   General Forrest turned to an orderly: "Go fetch Grissom here; tell him to come right away."   The surgeon soon came, General Forrest told Whistling Jim to lead the way, and we were soon riding through the night in the direction of the river.

III

A fine mist was falling, and the night was so dark that we would never have found our way but for a small dog whose inhospitable bark directed us to the cabin. The dog was so disturbed by our approach that a woman opened the door to see what the trouble could be. We found Jack Bledsoe on a pallet, and saw at a glance that the woman had administered such remedies as common-sense and experience had taught her would allay the fever of a wound. He recognized us at once, and Harry could hardly keep back his tears when he saw his college chum lying helpless on the floor. He supported Jack's head while the surgeon was examining the wound.

"You are here sooner than I thought," said Jack, gripping Harry's hand hard, "but I knew you would—I knew it. And there is Carroll Shannon," he went on, holding out a hand to me. "You never were very fond of me, Carroll, but I always liked you."

I hardly knew what to say, and therefore I said nothing. I could only take his hand in mine and give him a grip that would tell him more than words could tell. "Don't worry, old fellow," Jack continued, observing the expression of grief and anxiety in Harry Herndon's countenance. "It's all owing to the way the cards fall. Some day your turn may come, and then I hope I'll be able to go to you." His eyes were unnaturally bright, and his lips trembled with suppressed emotion.

The tension was relieved by the woman, who looked at both the young fellows, and then turned to the surgeon and asked almost unconcernedly, "Ain't war a hell of a thing?"

It was the surgeon who responded. "It would be hard to find a better definition, ma'am."

"I've saw lots wuss'n this," she remarked, as if she would thus find excuse for her sudden use of an expression that is rarely heard on the lips of a woman.

"Why, yes, ma'am—a great deal worse. This is not a bad case at all. No great damage has been done. He will be lame for some weeks— perhaps for a longer time. The ball struck the bone, glanced, and is now close to the surface."

In a few moments he had deftly extracted it, and the wounded man seemed to be greatly relieved. Medicine, strange to say, had been declared a contraband of war by the Federals, and the surgeon could spare but a driblet of quinine from his small supply; but he left some, and gave various directions with respect to the possible symptoms that might arise.

Just then the woman's husband entered the door. He was an emaciated, unkempt man, whose movements were in strange contrast with his appearance. He was one of the most trustworthy of General Forrest's scouts, but neither betrayed the fact that he knew the other. On the contrary, the man was both angry and rude. "What'd I tell you, Rhody?" he exclaimed, turning to his wife. "I know'd they'd crowd us out'n house an' home ef they got a chance; I could 'a' took oath to it! Cuss 'em, an' contrive 'em, both sides on 'em, all an' similar! They'd as lief make a hoss-stable out'n the house as not, an' I built it wi' my two han's."

"An' what ef you did?" inquired the woman

with some show of spirit. "Hit ain't sech a
beauty that you kin brag on it. An' who made
your two han's? You made 'em, I reckon, an'
nobody else could 'a' done it."

The man made a gesture as though he could
in that way weaken the force of the woman's
words, and he evidently knew when to speak, for
he said no more. On the contrary, sympathy
shone in his eyes when he looked at the wounded
man. "Don't you worry, Bill; ef ther's any
worryin' to be done, leave it to me. It takes a
'oman to know how to worry right; an' ever'thing
oughter be done right."

"Can you get a boat across the river?" inquired
General Forrest, turning to the man. He was
somewhat doubtful until he caught the General's
eye, and then he thought that nothing would be
easier. "Well," said the General, "go across
and tell the Yankees that there's a wounded
officer at your house and that he needs attention.
Tell 'em that General Forrest says they can get
him whenever they send after him."

"Is this General Forrest?" inquired Jack Bledsoe. "General, I hardly know how to thank
you. I had just been dreaming of prison."

The General made a deprecatory gesture, and was on the point of saying something, when the man of the house spoke up. "Ef you're Gener'l Forrest," he said, "you'll be more than pleased to know that the Yankees ain't never took time for to cook supper. After they hit the furder bank they jest kep' on a-humpin', an' I don't blame 'em myself, bekaze 'twuz the only way wet men could keep warm."

"It's up to you, Herndon; he's your prisoner. He ought to be in a hospital where he could be looked after, but I reckon he'll have to stay where he is for a while."

"He won't put me out a mite ef he stays," said the woman. "He'll be company fer me when Bill is pirootin' 'roun'."

General Forrest gave us permission to remain where we were for the night. "We move at five," said he. "Bill here will put you across and show you which way to go when he has found your horses for you." Just how Bill would do that was a mystery, but we asked no questions.

We called for Whistling Jim when General Forrest had gone, but he was nowhere to be found. He had shown us the way to the cabin and then disappeared. I judged that he was afraid Jack Bledsoe would upbraid him or that Harry would give him a scolding; but, whatever his reasons, he disappeared when we went in the cabin, and we saw him no more till the next morning.

Harry and Jack talked of old times until the woman was compelled to warn the wounded man that it would be worse for him if he excited himself. But he talked away in spite of the warning. He talked of his sister Katherine, much to Harry's delight, and told of his own sweetheart in Missouri. His colonel, he said, was very fond of Katherine, but he declared that Kate still thought of Harry, whereupon the young fellow blushed and looked as silly as a school-girl.

Tom Ryder was the Colonel's name, and he had a sister Lucy. Miss Lucy was Jack's choice out of a thousand, he said. The main trouble with Jack was that his sweetheart's sister, Jane Ryder, didn't like him—and so forth and so on, till I nodded where I sat, and dreamed of Katherine and Jane and Lucy Ryder, until someone took me by the arm and told me that it was time to be up and going.

We delayed our departure on one excuse and another, until finally Bill, who was to be our guide, grew irritable; and even then we made a further delay while Jack pencilled a note to his colonel, which Harry was to take charge of as long as there was danger of his capture by roving bands of Federals, and then it was to be given to the guide, who thought he could insure its delivery.

When we were ready, and could invent no further excuse, Harry turned to Jack. "The war doesn't touch us, dear boy. Good-by, and don't fail to put in a good word for me when you go home."

Jack Bledsoe's face brightened up. "That's so!" he exclaimed; "I can go home now. Well, you may depend on me, Harry; but the two Miss Ryders are all the other way, and I'll be between two fires. Tell Whistling Jim I have no hard feelings. He has really done me a favor, if things turn out no worse than they are."

We bade our friend good-by again and went out into the damp morning air, each with his various thoughts. I congratulated myself that mine had little to do with the troublesome sex. The fog, hanging heavily over the river, shut out the sunlight. We had to take the guide's word for that, for we could see no sign of the sun. Indeed, it was so dark that we had considerable difficulty in making our way. But when we were on the other side, and had mounted the somewhat steep bank, the fog disappeared and the sun shone out; and not far away we saw Whistling Jim and the horses.

He hailed our coming with delight, for he had been waiting some time, and he was both cold and frightened. He took off his hat, as he said, to old King Sun, and he seemed to feel all the better for it; and we all felt better when our horses were between our knees. Even the horses felt better, for they whinnied as we mounted, and were for going at a more rapid gait than was necessary.

We entered the scrub timber and went through it for half a mile or more, and then suddenly came out on the public highway. The guide suggested that we smarten up our gait, and we put the horses to a canter. I thought surely that the man would give out, but he merely caught hold of my stirrup to help him along, and when we came to a cross-road, and halted at his suggestion, he showed as little fatigue as the horses—this man who seemed too frail to walk a mile.

Here he gave us such instructions as seemed necessary, and was just about to so-long us, as he said, when he paused with his hand to his ear. "I'll be whopped," he exclaimed, "ef I don't hear buggy-wheels, an' they're comin' right this way." With that he slipped into the bushes, and, though I knew where he was concealed, it was impossible to catch a glimpse of him.

There was a bend in the road about a quarter of a mile ahead of us, and we waited expectantly, while Whistling Jim, with a cunning for which I did not give him credit, pretended to be fixing his saddle-girth. As we waited a top-buggy rounded the bend in the road and came bowling toward us. It was surprising to see a buggy, but I was more surprised when its occupant turned out to be a woman—a woman in a top-buggy, riding between two hostile armies!

IV

The lady made no pause whatever, and apparently was not at all surprised to find soldiers in the road ahead of her. She was not large, and yet she had a certain dignity of deportment. She was not youthful, neither was she old, but she was very grave-looking, as if she had seen trouble or was expecting to see it. Under any other circumstances I should have paid small attention to her, but the situation was such that I was compelled to regard her with both interest and curiosity. Almost in a moment my curiosity took the shape of sympathy, for there was something in the pale face that commanded it.

She was accompanied by a very clean-looking officer on horseback, and he, in turn, was followed by a small escort of cavalry—I did not take the trouble to count them, for my eyes were all for the lady; and it was left to Harry Herndon to realize the fact that we were in something of a pickle should the officer take advantage of the position in which he found us. He saw at once that our capture was a certainty unless we took prompt measures to provide against it, and he was quick to suggest that we adopt the tactics of Forrest and ride at them if they made a display of hostilities. I had just time to shift my carbine to the front under my overcoat and loosen the flap of my holsters when the lady drove up. We raised our hats as she came up, and made way for her to pass.

But she did nothing of the sort. She brought her horse to a halt. "Good-morning," she said, as cool as a cucumber. "You can't deceive us with your blue overcoats; you are both rebels. Oh, I have heard more of you Southerners than can be found in the newspapers."

"I'm sure we had no thought of deceiving you," responded Harry with one of his engaging smiles. "We are from the South, and you are from the North, of course. It may be that we are well met."

"Oh, no! not this time. I have seen prisoners taken before," remarked the lady with a little smile.

"Then you'll not flinch to see them taken again," said Harry very boldly. "But I shall regret to put you to any inconvenience."

I think the confident air of Harry saved us considerable trouble at the moment; but while he was putting on a bold front and trembling in his shoes—as he told me afterward—I had my eyes on the lady. She looked at me once, and turned her face away; twice, and frowned; thrice, and blushed. "I was afraid at first that you were a prisoner," I remarked in a tone that was intended to be apologetic, but the lady calmly turned her head away and ignored me.

"To what command are you attached?" inquired the Federal officer, very brusquely.

"We are serving under General Forrest," replied Harry.

"Why are you so far away from your command?" the officer inquired with real curiosity. His tone was so puzzling that Harry hesitated an instant—but in that instant a detachment of Forrest's troopers came around the bend in the road.

"Are we indeed so very far from our command?" I inquired.

The troopers came rattling up, and the officer turned to the lady, somewhat ungraciously, I thought, with the remark that they had been led into an ambuscade.

This was so ridiculous that I laughed aloud, though I felt little like laughing. "What amuses you?" the lady asked in some surprise. "I am sure I can see nothing humorous in our situation."

"Perhaps you have heard ladies placed under such accusations before?" I suggested.

"Miss Ryder knows I meant no such thing," said the officer with some heat.

"Is this Miss Lucy Ryder?" I inquired.

"What do you know of Lucy Ryder?" the lady asked.

"I know she has a sister Jane," I answered, whereupon the lady blushed again. "And I have heard that Miss Jane doesn't like a friend of ours —a young fellow named Jack Bledsoe, who is greatly in need of sympathy at this time."

"I like him well enough to go on a wild-goose chase in search of him," the lady replied. "We had an idea that he had been left on the battle-field."

Harry, who had been consulting with our comrades who had just arrived, returned in time to overhear a part of this conversation. He fumbled in his pocket and finally produced Jack Bledsoe's note. He lifted his hat as he handed it to the lady. She read it very calmly, and then passed it to the Federal officer who had escorted her: "You see, I am justified in coming."

"We sat up with Jack last night, my friend and I," Harry remarked.

"Well, you know the Bible tells us to love our enemies," remarked the lady, dryly.

"It was an easy matter to carry out the commandment in this particular instance, for, with the exception of this gentleman here"—indicating me—"Jack Bledsoe is the dearest friend I ever had."

"I know you well enough," the lady remarked with a smile. "You are Harry Herndon, and your friend there is Carroll Shannon, and the negro is Whistling Jim. Why, I know your grandmother, although I have never seen her."

"That doesn't help us now. How are we to find Captain Bledsoe?" asked the officer. I could have slapped him for the tone he employed.

"It is all provided for," replied Harry Herndon, curtly. "All you have to do is to hold on to the pommel of your saddle. There is a noncombatant here who will guide you. Bill!"

"I'm a-lis'nin' at ye," responded the guide from the bushes.

"This is one of the natives," Harry explained. "His wife is taking care of Jack Bledsoe and he will have no difficulty whatever in showing you the way."

The officer thanked us ungraciously, though why he took that attitude I was unable to discover, and we were on the point of joining our comrades when the lady remarked: "You'll probably know me again when you see me, Mr. Carroll Shannon!" This was a rebuke, I knew, and it upset me not a little, but there was something in the tone of her voice that sounded like a challenge, and I remarked that I should be sure to know her. "Then call my attention to the fact when you next see me," she cried as she touched up her horse.

"With great pleasure," I answered, raising my hat, and with that we were off to join our waiting comrades. It seemed that General Forrest was somewhat concerned for our safety, knowing that the country was strange to us, and he had sent William Forrest's company of Independents to watch the road for us so that we might come to no harm. While engaged in carrying out this order they saw the lady and her escort far ahead of them, and a detachment was sent to investigate, the rest of the company remaining to see whether other Federals would follow. Thus they came upon us in the very nick of time, for I judge that the Federal officer would have held us prisoners, in spite of the information we had for him, for he was very gruff and surly.

We reached the recruiting camp at Murfreesborough without further incident, and Harry and I soon settled down to the routine of duties that fell to our share. Harry served General Forrest temporarily as a courier, while I was billeted with Captain Bill Forrest's company of Independents, sometimes known as the Forty Thieves, owing to their ability as foragers.

I had time to ramble about in the woods, and I took advantage of it to explore the whole countryside in the neighborhood of the camp. Returning one day from a ride that was partly on business and partly for pleasure, I was informed that General Forrest had sent for me. When I responded to his summons he was reading a late copy of the Chattanooga *Rebel*, and was evidently much interested in what he read. He handed the paper to me when he had finished, and pointed out an article that was printed under a great display of black type.

A Federal scout, Leroy by name, and well known in both armies (so the newspaper said), had entered General Bragg's lines under very peculiar circumstances and had then managed to escape. Two pickets had been found bound and gagged. The whole story appeared to be absurd.

It was stated, among other things, that the scout intended to turn his attention to General Forrest. He directed my eye to this, and said he wanted me to take the matter in hand. I inquired how the correspondent knew the intentions of the scout.

"Why, he guessed 'em," replied General Forrest, "and he guessed right, too. I've got information from one of my men who is thick with

"I want you to catch this fellow and fetch him to me"

the Yankees that this chap will soon be nosing around here, and I want to give him the worth of his money. I don't want the other side to know how many men I've got, and I don't want 'em to know that my superior officer has refused to honor my requisition for arms and horses. I'd cut a purty figure with the Yankees if they know'd that some of my men had muskets that were used in the Revolutionary War. If they found this out I'd never whip another fight. And there's another thing: I don't want to have it said that any Yankee scout can stick his nose in my camp and not git it pulled. That's why I sent for you; I want you to catch this fellow and fetch him to me."

I tried hard to get out of the difficulty. I protested that I didn't know the scout from a side of sole leather. But the General said that this was one of his reasons for detailing me to perform this duty. He said he would have given it to Jasper Goodrum, of the Independents, but everybody in Tennessee knew Goodrum.

"He was born and raised around here," the General said, "and he's got a tongue like a bell-clapper. Now, you're not much of a talker, and your face gives you the look of a big baby that has got out of its mammy's yard and don't know how to git back." I suppose I must have turned red under this back-handed compliment, for he went on, "I wish I had a thousand like you. I watched you that day on the hill and at the river, and you may put it down that I'll trust you anywhere."

I tried to thank the General for his confidence, but he stayed me by a gesture. He settled all the details that could be thought of beforehand, and, as I turned to go, he rose from his chair and followed me to the door. "If you have to shoot that fellow," he said, "do it and don't wait too long before you do it; and if you have to shoot two or three men, don't let that stand in your way —charge 'em up to me. But you must catch that fellow; I want to string him up just to show the balance of 'em that they can't fool with me."

As everything had been arranged to my hand I was soon going about the camp and the town arrayed in jeans clothes and looking like anything but a soldier. I had thought to surprise Whistling Jim, the negro, with my garb, but, as it turned out, the surprise was mine, for that night, when I went to see whether the horses had been properly groomed and fed, I found the door of the stable unlocked. I was not only surprised but irritated. Both Harry Herndon and myself had tried hard to impress the negro with the necessity of taking unusual precautions to secure the safety of the horses, for they had attracted the attention of the whole camp, which was full of questionable characters, some of whom would have answered to their names if Falstaff had appeared to call the roll of his ragamuffins.

The key had been turned in the lock, but the bolt of the lock had failed to catch in the socket. It was plain that the negro thought he had locked the door, but it was quite as plain that he had been careless, and I made a resolution then and there to look after the safety of the horses myself. I swallowed more than half of my irritation when I found that the horses were in their stalls, warmly blanketed, and an abundance of food before them. I was on the point of locking the door with my own key, when I heard the sound of approaching footsteps. There were two men, civilians, as I judged, and one of them

stuttered. Their conversation was of a nature
to interest me.

They paused near the door of the stable.
"This is the place where they keep them," remarked one of the men. "They are the finest
horses in the rebel army, and it would be a good
job to run them into the Union lines some fine
night. I know a man that would pay a cracking
good price for them."

"But the nigger sleeps in there with 'em," said
the other man, "and what are you going to do
about him?"

"That's as easy as picking up rocks in the
road. A nigger will sell his immortal soul for
ten dollars, and I'll git him to leave the door open
some night when he's got a job of jiggering on
the peanner and whistling with his mouth at the
tavern in the woods."

"But that's horse-stealing."

"No, it ain't; it's turn and turn about. How
many horses has old Forrest took from the loyal
citizens of Tennessee? You couldn't count 'em
if you was to try. I'll give you three hundred
dollars for them three horses delivered at my
brother's house—three hundred dollars in gold—

and you'll have two men to help you. Don't you call that picking up money?"

"An' whilst I'm a-gittin' the horses, what'll you be doing?"

"Ain't I told you?" answered the man with some display of irritation. "I'll be putting up the money, the cold cash. What more do you want? I've always heard that good money is good enough for anybody."

They passed on, and I slipped from the stable, taking care to lock it behind me, and followed them.

V

I have never spent a more disagreeable hour than
that which passed while I was engaged in following the two men for the purpose of identifying
them. The weather was cold and the night dark,
and there were peppery little showers of sleet.
The two left the town proper and turned into a
by-way that I had travelled many times in my
rambles in the countryside. I knew that it led
to a house that had been built for a suburban
home, but now, in the crowded condition of the
town, was used as a tavern. It had attracted the
suspicion of General Forrest and I knew that
he had placed it under the surveillance of the
Independents. It was a very orderly public-
house, however, and nothing had ever occurred
there to justify the suspicions of the General.

The two men I followed could have reached
their destination in less than twenty minutes if
they had gone forward with the briskness that

the weather justified; but there was an argument of some kind between them—I judged that the stuttering man had no stomach for the part he was to play as a horse-thief. At any rate, there was a dispute of some kind, and they stopped on the road at least half a dozen times to have it out. One point settled, another would arise before they had gone far, and then they would stop again; and at last, so dark did the wood become, and so low their conversation grew, that I passed within three feet of them and never knew it until it was too late to betray the astonishment I naturally felt.

I simply jogged along the path and pretended that I had not seen them. I went along briskly, and in a few minutes came to the tavern. The door was shut, the weather being cold, but I knew by the lights shining through the windows that a hospitable fire was burning on the hearth. There was no need to knock at the door. I heard the jangling piano playing an accompaniment to the flute-like whistling of Harry Herndon's negro. Remembering his carelessness, I felt like going into the tavern and giving him a frailing. The inclination was so strong that I held my hand on the door-knob until the first flush of anger had subsided. It was a very fortunate thing for me, as it turned out, that Whistling Jim was present, but at the moment the turn of a hair would have caused me to justify much that the people of the North have said in regard to the cruelty of Southerners to the negro.

The guests and visitors—and there were quite a number—made room for me at the fire, the landlord provided me with a chair and welcomed me very heartily, taking it for granted that I was from the country and would want a bed for the night. On the wide hearth a very cheerful fire burned, and the place reminded me somehow of home—particularly a big rocking-chair in which one of the guests was seated. It had an upholstered seat and back, and the high arms were made more comfortable by a covering of the same material. It was a fac-simile of a chair that we had at home, and I longed to occupy it, if only for the sake of old times.

Among those who were taking their ease at this suburban inn was Jasper Goodrum, one of my comrades. He was a noted scout as well as a seasoned soldier. He looked at me hard as I entered, and continued to watch me furtively for some time, and then his face cleared up and I knew that he had recognized me. He was in civilian's clothes, and I knew by that that he did not care to be recognized. So I turned my attention elsewhere. But in a little while he seemed to have changed his mind, and, suddenly rising from his chair, came to me with outstretched hand.

It was a mixed company around the fire. There was a big Irishman, who leaned calmly back in a small chair and smoked a short pipe. More than once I caught his bright eyes studying my face, but his smile was ample apology for his seeming rudeness. He was as handsome a man as I had ever seen, and if I had been searching for a friend on whom to depend in an emergency I should have selected him out of a thousand.

There was a short-haired man who was built like a prize-fighter. He wore a sarcastic smile on his face, and his shifty eyes seemed to be constantly looking for a resting-place. He had a thick neck and jaw like a bull-dog. I marked him down in my mental note-book as dangerous. There was a tall and pious-looking man, and two or three civilians who had no particular points about them; and then there was a burly man, who sat with his hands in his pockets and did nothing but chew tobacco and gaze in the fire, uttering not one word until some of the company fell to discussing Captain Leroy, the famous Union scout. When Leroy's name was mentioned the burly man was quick to join in the conversation.

"There ain't a word of truth in all this stuff you hear about Leroy," he said, and his manner was more emphatic than the occasion seemed to demand. "He's in the newspapers, and he ain't anywhere else on top of the ground. I know what I'm a-talking about. Leroy is the invention of Franc Paul, of the Chattanooga *Rebel*. He as good as told me so. He said that when he wanted to stir up talk and create a sensation he had something written about this Captain Frank Leroy. He's a paper man and he's able to do anything the newspapers want done."

"You talk like you had gray hair," said the man that looked like a prize-fighter; "but you're givin' away a mighty big secret. What are you doin' it for? Say!"

"Oh, because I'm tired of all this talk about a man that doesn't live outside of the mind of a newspaper man."

The big Irishman, who had been smoking and watching me with a shrewd smile hovering about his mouth, began to chuckle audibly. He kept it up so long that it attracted the attention of the company.

"What tickles you, my friend?" the burly man asked.

"Maybe ye know Franc Paul?" he inquired. His countenance was an interrogation-point. The man answered somewhat sullenly in the affirmative. "Is there anny risimblance bechune him an' me?"

"Not the slightest in the world," the man answered.

"Thin ye'd have a quarrel wit' his wife an' she'd have all the advantages," said the Irishman with a laugh. "F'r no longer than the last time I was at Chattanooga, Missus Paul says, 'It's a good thing, Mr. O'Halloran,' she says, 'that ye're a hair's breadth taller than me beloved husband,' she says, 'or I'd niver tell ye apart. Only the sharp eyes av a wife or a mither,' she says, 'could pick out me husband if he stood be your side,' she says."

"I must say," remarked the pious-looking man, "that you gentlemen were never more mistaken in your lives when you hint that there is no such person as Frank Leroy. I knew him when he was a boy—a beardless boy, as you may say. In fact, his father was my next-door neighbor in Knoxville, and I used to see Frank reading old Brownlow's paper."

"Don't think ut!" replied the Irishman, and with that all joined in the conversation and I heard more of the perilous adventures and hair-breadth escapes of Captain Frank Leroy than you could put in a book. It seemed that his identity was a mystery, but he was none the less a hero in men's minds because his very existence had been called in question; for people will hug delusions to their bosoms in the face of religion itself, as we all know.

The door of an inner room was open, and I could hear a conversation going on. One of the participants was the stuttering man, whose voice I had heard before the stable-door, and at a moment when I thought that my movements would

attract no attention I took advantage of the free-
dom of a public-house and sauntered aimlessly
into the room as if I had no particular business
there. I saw with surprise that the chap who
had proposed to steal the horses was one of the
merchants of the town at whose store I had occa-
sionally traded. In the far end of the room,
reading a newspaper by the light of a small fire,
sat a slip of a youth. He wore a military cloak
that covered his figure from his neck to his top-
boots.

I saw that he was not so absorbed in the paper
that he failed to make a note of my presence in
the room, and he shifted himself around in his
chair so that he could get a better view of me, and
still leave his face in the shadow. Near him sat
a motherly-looking woman of fifty. She was
well preserved for her age, and wore a smile on
her face that was good to look at. The youngster said something to her in a low tone, and she
immediately turned her attention to me. Some
other words passed between the two, and then the
woman beckoned to me. I obeyed the summons
with alacrity, for I liked her face.

"You seem to be lonely," she said. "Have a

seat by our little fire. This is not a guest-room, but we have been so overrun lately that we have had to turn it over to the public." She paused a moment and then went on. "You are over-young to be in the army," she suggested.

She had turned so that she looked me full in the face, and there was a kindly, nay, a generous light in her eyes, and I could no more have lied to her in the matter than I could have lied to my own mother if she had been alive. "I do not have a very hard time in the army," I replied.

"No, I suppose not," she remarked. "You are one to make friends wherever you go. Few are so fortunate; I have known only one or two."

There was a note of sadness in her tones that touched me profoundly. The cause I can't explain, and the effect was beyond description. I hesitated before making any reply, and when I did I tried to turn it off lightly. "I never saw but one," I answered, "on whom I desired to make an impression."

"And who was that?" the woman inquired with a bright smile of sympathy.

"You will think it a piece of foolishness," I replied; "but it was a lady riding in a top-buggy. I had never seen her before and never expect to see her again."

The youngster clutched his paper in his hand and turned in his chair. "The light is detestable," he said. "Please throw on a piece of pine, mother."

"You can't read by such a light," the woman replied. "Put your paper in your pocket and read it to-morrow." Then she turned to me. "If you are in the army," she said, "why do you wear such clothes? They are not becoming at all." She had such a kindly smile and betrayed such a friendly interest that it was not in human nature to suspect her—at least, it was not in my nature to do so.

"Why, mainly for comfort," I answered; "and while I am wearing them I am having my uniform, such as it is, furbished up and cleaned a bit. I have a few days' leave, and I am taking advantage of it in this way."

"I wish my son here would take advantage of his short furlough to wear the clothes he used to wear," she remarked, and her tone was so significant that I could but regard her with a look of inquiry. I suppose the puzzled expression of my face must have amused her, for she laughed heartily, while the son, as if resenting his mother's words, arose and swaggered to the other end of the room.

We had more conversation, and then I returned to the public room. Some of the guests had retired, but their places had been taken by others, and there was a goodly company gathered around the fire. I found the big arm-chair unoccupied, and, seating myself on its comfortable cushion, soon forgot the wonder I had felt that the woman in the next room had known me for a soldier. I had accomplished one thing—the identification of the prospective horse-thief—and I satisfied myself with that. As for Leroy, I knew I should have to trust to some stroke of good fortune.

The comfort of the rocker appealed to me, and, with my hands on its arms, I leaned back and, in spite of the talking all around me, was soon lost in reflection. Through long usage the upholstering on the arms of the chair had become worn, and in places the tufts of moss or horsehair were showing. I fell to fingering these with the same impulse of thoughtlessness that induces people to bite their finger-nails. Suddenly I felt my finger in contact with a small roll of paper that had been carefully pushed under the leather, and then I remembered that the last occupant of the chair was the short-haired man—the man who had the general appearance of a prize-fighter.

Now, it had occurred to me in a dim way that this man might be identical with Leroy, and I suspected that he had left in the chair a communication for some of his accomplices. I determined to transfer the roll of paper to my pocket and examine it at my leisure. But no sooner had I come to this determination than I imagined that every person in the room had his eyes fixed on me. And then the problem, if you can call it so, was solved for me.

A stranger who had evidently arrived while I was in the next room appeared to be regarding Whistling Jim with some curiosity, and presently spoke to him, inquiring if he was the negro that played on the piano. Whistler replied that he could "sorter" play. "If you are Whistling

Jim," I said, "play us a plantation tune. I heard a man say the other day that the finest tune he ever heard was one you played for him. It was something about 'My gal's sweet.'"

The negro looked at me hard, but something in my countenance must have conveyed a warning to him. "I 'member de man, suh; he say he wuz fum Cincinnati, an' he gun me a fi'-dollar bill—a green one."

Without more ado, he went to the piano and plunged into the heart-breaking melody of—

> "Yo' gal's a neat gal, but my gal's sweet—
>   Sweet-a-little, sweet-a-little, sweet, sweet, sweet!
> Fum de crown er her head ter de soles er her feet—
>   Feet-a-little, feet-a-little, feet, feet, feet!"

Naturally all eyes were turned on the performer, and I took advantage of that fact to rise from the rocking-chair with the roll of paper safe in my pocket, and saunter across the room in the direction of the piano. Leaning against a corner of the ramshackle old instrument, I drank in the melody with a new sense of its wild and melancholy beauty. The room in which I stood seemed transformed into what it never could be, and the old piano shed its discord and was glorified by the marvellous playing of the negro.

The foolish little song runs along for several stanzas, simulating the sound of dancing feet. Alternately the negro sang the air and whistled the chorus, but whether he did one or the other, the effect was the same. The silly song struck the home note and sent it vibrating through my brain so invitingly that I was almost sorry that Whistling Jim had played it.

I returned to earth when he ceased playing. He looked hard at me when he had finished, but I did not glance at him. At the other end of the piano, leaning against it, and apparently lost in thought, was the young fellow I had seen in the other room. His cloak was thrown back from his throat, and the red lining gave a picturesque touch to his small, lithe figure. His face was partly in the shadow, but I could see that his expression was one of profound melancholy. He aroused himself at last, and, looking toward me, said with a smile that had no heart in it, "If all the negroes in the South are so gifted you must have a happy time down there."

"So it would seem," I answered, "but this negro is an exception. He tells me that he learned to play while his old mistress was away from home looking after her plantation interests. He can whistle better than he can play."

"He has great gifts," said the lad, "and I trust he is treated accordingly; but I doubt it," and with that he turned away from the piano with a snap of thumb and finger that sounded for all the world like a challenge. He turned and went swaggering across the room, and seated himself in the rocking-chair of which I have spoken. In a word, and with a snap of the finger, he had thrown mud at the whole South, and with no more excuse than I should have had had I made an attack on the North. Yet curiosity, and not irritation, was uppermost in my mind.

His conduct was so puzzling that I determined to have another taste of it if possible, and so discover what he would be at. So I went back to the fire and took a seat close to his elbow, while Whistling Jim passed around his hat, as was his custom when he played for company. He held it out to all except the young fellow and myself, and then returned to the piano and played for his own amusement, but so softly that conversation could flow on undisturbed.

I had a good look at the lad, and liked him all the better. His face had in it that indescribable quality—a touch of suffering or of sorrow—that always draws me, and I thought how strange it was that he should sit there ignorant of the fact that a word or two would make me his friend for life. I had a great pity for him, and there arose in me the belief that I had met him before, but whether in reality or only in a dream I could not make out. It was a foolish and a romantic notion, but it nibbled around my mind so persistently that I turned my gaze on the fire and fell into reflections that were both teasing and pleasing.

While thus engaged I suddenly became aware of the fact that the young fellow was fingering at the worn place on the chair-arm. Conversation was going on very briskly. The genial landlord, who had joined the group at the fire, was relating to a listening and an eager guest another story of the almost superhuman performances of the Union scout, Leroy, when suddenly the lad arose from the rocker and began to search the floor with his eyes. He had had the color of youth in his cheeks, in spite of the swarthiness of his skin, and I had admired the combination—your light-haired man is for everything that has a touch of the brunette—but now he had gone white.

As he stooped to search under my chair, I jumped up and drew it back politely. "Pardon me for disturbing you," he said; "I have lost a paper."

"Is it of importance?" I inquired, endeavoring to show an interest in the matter.

"You would hardly think so," he replied. "It involves the safety of a woman." I regarded him with unfeigned astonishment, and he, in turn, looked at me with a face as full of anger and disappointment as I had ever beheld.

"Why, you young rascal!" I exclaimed; "what do you know of me that you should speak so? For less than nothing I'll give you a strapping and send you to your daddy."

"You couldn't do me a greater service. He is in heaven." You may imagine my feelings, if you can, when, as he said this, he turned toward me a countenance from which all feeling had died out save that of sadness. If he had plunged a knife in my vitals he could not have hurt me worse. "Well, sir," he insisted, "proceed with your strapping."

"You are more than even with me, my lad," I said, "and I humbly apologize for my words. But why should you be so short with one who certainly wishes you no harm?"

"I am unable to tell you. You seem to be always smiling, while I am in trouble: perhaps that is why I am irritable." He looked at me hard as he resumed his seat in the rocker, and again I had the curious feeling that I had met him somewhere before—perhaps in some sphere of former existence. Memory, however, refused to disgorge the details, and I could only gaze helplessly into the fire.

After a little the lad hitched his chair closer to mine, and I could have thanked him for that. He drew on his glove and drew it off again. "Will you shake hands with me?" he inquired. "I feel that I am all to blame." As I took his hand in mine I could but notice how small and soft it was.

"No, you are not all to blame," I said.   "I am
ill-mannered by nature."

"I never will believe it," he declared with something like a smile.   "No, it is not so."

Before I could make any reply, in walked Jasper Goodrum, of the Independents, and, following hard at his heels, was the man who had the
appearance of a prize-fighter.   This last comer
appeared to be in a state of great excitement, and
his brutal, overbearing nature was clearly in evidence.   He walked across the room to my lad—
I was now beginning to feel a proprietary interest in him—and seized him roughly by the
arm.

"Come 'ere!" he said, and his voice was thick
with anger.   "You've got more'n you bargained
for.   Come into the next room; you better had!
Say, ain't you comin'?"   He tried to pull the lad
along, but the youngster was not to be pulled.

"Don't touch me!" he exclaimed.   "Don't you
dare to put your hands on me.   You have lied to
me, and that is enough!"   The short-haired man
was almost beside himself with anger, and I could
see that the lad would be no match for him.   He
was not at all frightened, but when he turned his

eyes toward me, with a little smile, I saw the face of Jane Ryder, the little lady I had seen in a top-buggy on her way to carry aid to Jack Bledsoe. And instantly I was furious with a blind rage that stung me like a thousand hornets.

I rose and slapped the ruffian on the shoulder in a way that would have knocked an ordinary man down. "You dirty brute!" I cried, "say to me what you have to say to the lad!"

VI

The man regarded me with an amazement that soon flamed up into anger. His under-jaw stuck out ferociously, and the veins on his neck and forehead were swollen with indignation. Before he could say anything Jasper Goodrum intervened. "This is partly my affair," he said to the short-haired man, "and you'd better leave this countryman alone."

"You're wrong," said the man; "it is not your affair. How can it be when I don't know you?"

"Still," insisted Goodrum, "you'd better not bother the countryman. You'll git yourself in trouble."

"Trouble!" he snorted. "Say! that's what I'm after. He's waded into the creek and he can't git out without wettin' his feet." Then he turned to me, his eyes full of venomous rage. "Say! what do you take me for?" He came closer and stuck his ugly mug near my face.

Whistling Jim ran into him head down like a bull

My reply was made with an exceedingly will-ing mind. I struck him on the jaw with my open hand and sent him reeling. He recovered his balance almost instantly and made at me with a roar of rage and pain, but he never reached me, for Whistling Jim ran into him head down like a bull. The result was a collision that put the man out of business and knocked all the fight out of him. He lay on the floor and rolled about in an agony of pain, and the negro stood over him, apparently waiting for a fitting opportunity to put in the finishing touch, but his hard head had done the work for the time being.

I judged that the ruffian had friends among the guests, but when I turned to keep an eye on them the room was clear. Even the landlord had retired. The lad was standing by my side, and my impression is that he was holding me by the sleeve of my coat. I turned to him, and I was more certain than ever that he was either Jane Ryder or her brother. But it was only when she spoke again that I was sure—for not even a twin brother could simulate that round and singularly mellow voice. "I am afraid you have made matters somewhat hard for me," she said, somewhat sadly, "and heaven knows that I have had trouble enough for one night."

"Well, you will have no more trouble here, at any rate," I said.

"I'd feel easier if I were sure of that," she remarked.

"Be assured," I answered. "When I leave this house you will go with me. I propose to take you to your friends, if you have any in the neighborhood; otherwise you go with me. You shall not stay here for that ruffian to abuse and misuse you."

"I'll go with you as far as the door if only to thank you for the unnecessary protection you have given me. There are many things that you do not understand."

"And many that I do," I replied as significantly as I dared. "I want no thanks, and you shall not remain in this house to-night. That is settled." She made a birdlike movement with her head and shoulders, looked me up and down, and smiled, but she saw that I was in earnest, and the smile left her face.

"Where shall I go?" she asked.

"Anywhere but here," I answered. "Anywhere away from that," I pointed to the man on the floor. He had raised himself to a sitting posture, and was rocking himself to and fro with his arms hugging his knees, apparently in great pain.

"He is not always as you see him to-night," she insisted. Then she turned to me impulsively, "I'll go with you; I know a house where I have very dear friends. But I must tell my friend here good-night—the lady you spoke with." She ran into the inner room, and then I heard her going lightly upstairs. She came down in a moment with color in her face and with some agitation in her manner. She seized me by the sleeve in a way that no man would have thought of, exclaiming, "Let us go at once—come!" Her sudden anxiety to be off took me entirely by surprise.

"You have a horse?" I said, hearing the jingling of her spurs. But she declared that her horse was well enough off where he was. "Come!" she said; "let us be off!"

"With all my heart," I replied. I was so highly elated that I forgot for the moment that I was dealing with a woman, and I threw my arm lightly over her shoulder with a gesture of friendliness and protection.

She threw it off and shrank from it as if it were a serpent. "What do you mean?" she cried. Her face was red with anger, and her eyes were blazing with scorn. "Don't dare to touch me!" For an instant I knew not what to do or say, and then it suddenly occurred to me that it would be well to hide from her the fact that I knew who she was and so I made a great pretence of anger. I seized her by the arm. "If you give me another word of your impertinence I'll carry out my threat of half an hour ago."

All the anger died out of her eyes. "You hurt me," she said almost in a whisper. "Oh, pray pardon me; I have travelled far to-day, and I am weak and nervous. Why did you come here to-night? But for you—" she paused and glanced up into my face, and placed her hand on mine. And then I would have known if I had not known before that she was no other than Jane Ryder, the little lady of the top-buggy. I looked in her eyes, and they fell; in her face, and it was covered with blushes; and somehow I was happier than I had been in many a long day.

"Come!" said I with some sternness, and held out my hand to her. Instinctively she seized it and clung to it as we went out into the night, followed by Whistling Jim.

"I have a friend who lives farther up the road," she said. "It is not far, but perhaps it is farther than you care to come—and you have no overcoat." I was not thinking of what she was saying, but of the warm little hand that nestled so confidingly in mine. I knew then, or thought I knew, that this little hand so soft and white, nestling in my big paw like a young bird under its mother's wing, had the power to make or mar my life. But, as is ever the way with birdlike things, the hand slipped from its nest and left it empty.

She was worrying about the ruffian we had left on the floor. "The trouble with him," I said, "is that he is selling information to both sides. He is an impostor. I think he is the scout they call Leroy." Whereupon she gave utterance to a laugh so merry that it sounded out of place in the gloomy woods. It brought Whistling Jim alongside to see what the trouble was. He said he thought the young master was crying. She laughed again, and then suddenly paused.

"We are very near the house," she said, "and all who live there are my friends. I shall be perfectly safe there. You have been very kind to me—kinder than you know. We have both seen each other at our very worst. Should we meet again, I hope we shall appear to better advantage."

She had entirely recovered her self-possession, but in doing so she forgot the part she was playing, forgot that she was arrayed in the toggery of a man, and was now altogether a woman. I do not remember all that was said, but I tried as hard as I could to conceal from her the fact that I had discovered her sex and her identity; I had not the least desire to humiliate her by airing my penetration. She stood silent for a while, as if in thought, or perhaps she was waiting for me to say farewell.

"You will do well to go in," I said. "The night is cold and damp."

"The cold and the damp are nothing to me," she replied. "I am warm enough. You were speaking a while ago of Frank Leroy. Don't forget that he is the best friend I have in the world except my mother. Good-night!" She held out her hand, and again it nestled, white and soft and warm, in my great paw, and stayed there a moment. The little hand must have been frightened, for it fluttered slightly and then flew back to its mistress.

I said good-night, but it was not a very gracious farewell, I am afraid. "I knew I had something to say to you," she remarked. "In the house there is a young Federal officer who was wounded some time ago. He has been in a very bad way, but he is better now. While he was at the worst of his illness he was constantly calling the names of some friends he has among the rebels. One of them he seems to be specially fond of—he calls him Harry Herndon. The other he calls Carroll Shannon. It may be that you know them."

"I am acquainted with Herndon," I replied. "Shannon I have never met, and I have no desire to meet him."

She was silent a moment, and then went on: "I thought that if the two would take the trouble to call on the wounded man it would do him good

—though I am astonished that he should desire to see rebels and traitors. I hate them all without exception, and the more I see of them the more I hate them."

The little lady had worked herself into a grand fury against the rebels, and I am sure she believed what she said for the moment. "I shall take pleasure in informing Herndon that his friend is here," said I. "Shannon, as I have told you, I never met."

"You are fortunate," she replied. "I met him once, and it needed only a glance to tell me what he was."

"And what was he?" I inquired.

"The matter is not worth speaking of," she said. "I have just as much contempt for him as you have. Good-night!" and once more the little fluttering hand touched mine, and away she marched into the darkness. At the steps she turned and listened, but, as neither Whistling Jim nor I had stirred out of our tracks, she could hear nothing. "Why don't you go?" she called.

"I want to see you safe in the house," I said.

"You are taking a deal of responsibility on

yourself," she responded. "You must think me a child or a woman." With that she slipped through the door, which yielded to her touch, and disappeared in the house.

VII

Now, when the foolish girl disappeared behind the door, I turned away from the gate full of anger at all mundane things. But the only human being near at hand was Whistling Jim, and him I seized by the collar.

"You scoundrel!" I exclaimed, shaking him vigorously; "what do you mean by going off and leaving the stable-door unlocked?"

"Mar—Marse Cal—Cally—lem—lemme tell you 'bout it!" he cried, affrighted; and then, ashamed of my silly display of temper, I turned him loose. "What make you so fractious ter-night, Marse Cally? A little mo' an' you'd 'a' shuck my head off. I declar' ter gracious, Marse Cally, I thought I locked dat stable-door. I know I turned de key—dey ain't no two ways 'bout dat. I tuck de key out'n de lock when I went in, an' put it back in de lock when I come out—I put it in de lock an' turned it des like I allers do."

"But what you didn't do," said I, now angry

with myself, "was to make sure that the bolt of
the lock had caught. It didn't catch, and when
I went there to-night the door yielded to my
hand. It was a piece of pure carelessness, and
if you ever do the like again——"

"Don't talk dat way, Marse Cally; you sho is
been mighty good ter me, an' I don't want ter
make you mad. I never is ter do dat trick
ag'in."

Then I told him that there was a plot on foot
to steal the horses, and advised him as to the
identity of the two men. He knew them both—
especially did he know the prominent citizen,
who, on various occasions, had invited him into
the store and made him presents of pipe and
tobacco, and had even hinted to him that he could
find a good job for him when he grew tired of
working for nothing. He had also given him
whiskey, which was a contraband article in the
recruiting camp.

We walked along very friendly, for I was
ashamed of myself for giving way to my temper.
When the negro thought I was in a sufficiently
good humor, he endeavored to ease his own
curiosity on a matter that had evidently been

worrying him. "Marse Cally," he said, "who wuz dat little chap we tuck home des now?"

"I don't know his name. Why do you ask?"

"Kaze he look so funny an' done so funny. He ain't look like no man ter me."

"Why, of course not; he is little more than a boy; that's the reason I made him come out of that house."

"He moughter been a boy," remarked Whistling Jim, after taking some time to think the matter over. "He wuz right knock-kneed, an' when he walked he walked des like de flo' wuz burnin' his foots."

I could only pretend to laugh, but I wondered at the negro's keep observation. Seeing that I made no reply, he went on: "You know what I think, Marse Cally? Dat uppity li'l chap is des ez much a man ez you is a 'oman."

"Well, it may be so," I replied. "He is nothing to me."

Whistling Jim laughed one of his irritating laughs. "Dat's so, suh, but I tuck notice dat you helt han's wid 'im a mighty long time."

This was intolerable, and I remarked with some severity that I proposed to make it my spe-

cial business to inform Harry Herndon how his
negro had neglected his duty. "Now, don't do
dat, Marse Cally, please, suh! You know
mighty well dat Marse Harry can't keep his
temper like you does. I dunner when you been
ez fractious ez you is ter-night."

"You are the cause of it," I declared, "you and
no one else. First you leave the stable-door unlocked, and then you say that this young fellow
is neither man nor boy."

"Did I say dat, Marse Cally?" exclaimed
Whistling Jim, apparently almost as much
amazed as if I had drawn a pistol on him. He
stood a moment, as if trying to remember the circumstances under which the remark had been
made, but he shook his head sadly. "Ef I said
dat, Marse Cally, I must 'a' been dreamin'; I wuz
mighty nigh fast asleep when we started back des
now, an' ef you'd 'a' lissened right close I speck
you'd 'a' hearn me a sno'in'. Ef you say I said
it, den I reckon I must 'a' said it, but I wan't at
myse'f, kaze ef dey ever wuz a grown man on top
er de groun', dat chap is one."

"You are sharper than I thought you were," I
remarked.

"You must be makin' fun er me, Marse Cally, kaze dey ain't nothin' sharp 'bout knowin' a man fum a 'oman. Ef I didn't know de diffunce I'd turn myse'f out ter graze wid de dry cattle, an' stay wid um all thoo de season."

"Now, that's the way to talk," said I with some heartiness; "but if I ever find the stable-door unlocked again I'll take it for granted that you have changed your opinion about our young friend."

"I may leave de stable-door onlocked time an' time ag'in," remarked Whistling Jim solemnly, "but I never is ter b'lieve dat dat boy is anything but a man."

I made haste to inform Harry Herndon that Jack Bledsoe was in the neighborhood, and, as was perfectly natural, he was keen to see him, less for Jack's sake, I imagine, though he loved the young fellow well, than for the sake of having some news of the fair Katherine. As the heaviest part of his work at headquarters was over, and as pretty much everything had depended on the reply to General Forrest's requisition on his superior officer—who, unfortunately, chanced to be General Bragg—for arms and ammunition, Harry had no difficulty in securing leave of absence for the day; and so, when all the arrangements had been made, we set out the next evening for the house where Jack Bledsoe lay.

On the way, I suggested that perhaps Jack's mother and the fair cousin would probably be found there; and this possibility was in Harry's mind also, for he leaned from his horse toward me and extended his hand, uttering not a word. I gripped it with mine, and hoped that before I died I should have the opportunity of shaking another hand as true. One other I found—but only one.

Jack's mother met us at the door, and not far behind her was the fair Katherine, more beautiful than ever. I saw at a glance that the ladies were expecting us, for they were rigged out in their best, which was not very bad, considering that they had been caught between the lines with a wounded man on their hands. Another face that I had expected to see was not in evidence, and whatever enthusiasm I may have felt in the beginning soon died away, and I was sorry that I had been foolish enough to accompany Harry.

We were taken at once to Jack's room, and it was very evident that he was glad to see us again. He had changed a great deal; he looked older, and appeared to be worn by illness. He had been removed from the cabin on the river at a critical period, and, as a result, he was compelled to go through a long and drastic illness. He was on the high road to recovery, but I thought he would never be the same handsome Jack again, so cadaverous was his countenance and so changed his voice. The two ladies and myself left the friends together and went into the room that had been the parlor, where there was a brisk fire burning.

The house was a very commodious country home and had evidently been built by some prosperous person whose heart and mind turned to the country after he had acquired wealth in the town. But the owner had deserted it when the Federals took possession of Murfreesborough, leaving furniture and everything to the mercy of circumstance—the cruel circumstance that goes hand in hand with war. But everything was intact. The old piano stood in the corner as glossy as if it had been newly bought, and the carpets on the floor wore a clean look, though some of them were threadbare.

After a while, Harry came in search of Kate —she was more important than his wounded friend—and Mrs. Bledsoe went to take her place by Jack's bedside. This arrangement would have left me very much alone, but for the thoughtfulness of Kate, who intimated that I should find very interesting company in the next room. "Don't be afraid," she said. But I was very much afraid, I know not why, and hesitated a long time before I ventured into the room.

And when I did venture to wander in casually, I was more afraid than ever, for at a window a small lady sat reading. I knew her at once for Jane Ryder, but that fact made me no bolder. On the contrary, I felt a timidity that was almost childish; it was a feeling that carried me away back to my boyhood, when I refused to go into a room where there was a company of little girls.

"I beg your pardon," said I, and began to back toward the door.

"Oh, no harm is done," the lady declared, closing the book, but keeping the place with her forefinger. "Did you desire to see me? Or perhaps you would see Miss Bledsoe?"

"No, ma'am—I—that is, Miss Bledsoe is talking with a friend of mine, and I just wandered in here, having nothing else to do."

"To be sure! I believe that is a custom of Southern gentlemen."

"What is?" I asked, rather abruptly.

"Why, to go to houses and wander from room to room until their curiosity is satisfied."

I was angry, though I knew that she meant not a word she said. "Does Mrs. Bledsoe indulge in that habit?" I asked.

"Habit? I said custom. Mrs. Bledsoe is a changed woman since she has lived among people who know something of the world and its ways, and who are not slave-drivers."

"I believe this is Miss Jane Ryder," I said.

"Your memory is better than your manners," she replied, and though I tried hard to keep my temper, her words stung me to the quick.

"I assure you I had not the least desire to disturb you. I came in here with the hope, though not the expectation, of finding a lad who came here last night."

"He is not here," she asserted, "and if he were, he has no desire to see you. He told me something of his encounter with you, and if that is the way you treat a young lad, I wonder how you would have treated an unprotected woman."

I would not trust myself to speak to her. I made her a low obeisance and retired from the room; but I was not to escape so easily. She pursued her advantage; she followed me out into the hall. "Is it true that the young man compelled you to accompany him to this house last night?"

"If he told you so, madam, it is true," I replied.

"After threatening to give you a strapping?" she asked. Her mood was almost exultant, though she had been gloomy enough when I first disturbed her.

"If he says so, madam."

"He didn't say so, but I believe he slapped your face, for it is still red."

"Perhaps he did, madam."

"I am no madam, I'll let you know; why do you call me so?"

"It is simply a term of respect, ma'am. Our

young people are taught to be respectful to ladies."

"You may be sure that the young man would have remained to see you, but I was afraid you'd run away and leave your friend." Women can be very childish sometimes, and this was pure childishness.

"Why, I had no idea that he bore me any ill-will," I remarked. "He trotted along by my side in perfect good-humor when I was fetching him home. If he has any grudge against me, I do not think the fault is mine. Say to him that I apologize most humbly for any offence I may have given him." Jane Ryder was now sure that I did not connect her with the lad—was sure that I had not pierced her disguise, and she became at once very much friendlier. Her relief was apparent in voice and gesture.

"The truth is," she went on, "the young man is very fond of you, much to my surprise. It is a strange fancy," she mused; "there is no accounting for it. I believe you could prevail on him to leave his friends and go with you to the South; that is why I am keeping him away from you."

"I have had few friends," I said, "and if you could add the young man to the list and place him above all the rest, I should be happy. But as for persuading him to desert his principles, I should never think of it; and I should think ill of him if he could be persuaded."

"He really thinks that you are one of the finest men he ever met," pursued Jane Ryder. "He says that a young woman would be as safe from insult with you as she would be with her mother."

"And why not?" I inquired. "I thank your friend for his good opinion of me; but it is no great compliment to me to say that I should protect a woman with my life, if need be. Back yonder there are gathered three or four thousand men, and out of that four thousand you will not find ten who would not do the same and think it nothing to boast of."

"I wouldn't trust them," she declared.

"Would you trust me?" I asked. The words were out of my mouth before I could recall them. They meant more than she would think or than she would care for them to mean.

"I certainly would," she said, clenching her hands in a strange little gesture.

"I thank you for saying that much," I declared. "The time may come—not soon, perhaps—when I shall have to ask you to trust me."

"Soon or late," she replied, "my answer will be the same."

I never was more shaken with the excitement of temptation than at that moment. She must have known it; they say women are quick at reading the thoughts of a man, but, instead of drawing away from me, she drew nearer. In another instant I should have seized her in my arms, the pale and lonely creature, but just then the sound of footsteps came along the hall, and I heard the happy laughter of Katherine Bledsoe. I had raised my arms, but now I lowered them and she had seized my hand.

"Good-by!" she said, and as soon as she could tear her hand from mine she was gone—gone by another door, and Harry and her companion came plump upon me standing in the hallway, gazing at the door through which Jane Ryder had disappeared. Then I turned and gazed at them, first at one and then at the other.

"What have you done with her?" inquired Kate, with just a shade of solicitude in her voice.

"Oh, I hope you haven't hurt her," she cried. "She has the tenderest heart in the world."

"Hurt her? Hurt her?" It was all that I could say, and then all of a sudden I came to myself and stood there laughing very foolishly. "She ran away," I explained. "I don't know why. I am sure I didn't want her to go!"

Whereupon Kate fell to laughing, and kept it up until the tears came into her eyes. "Oh, men are such simpletons!" she exclaimed; "I don't know what I should do for amusement if I didn't see the lords of creation once in a great while."

We bade good-by to the household—though Jane Ryder was nowhere to be found—and went to our horses, which we had left in charge of Whistling Jim. That worthy was in quite a flutter. He had heard strange noises, and he was almost sure that he had caught a glimpse of more than one man in the darkness. We paid little enough attention to what he said, for we knew that the ladies were safe so far as the Confederates were concerned, and Jack Bledsoe would answer for their safety with the Federals.

Nevertheless, there was no one to answer for

our safety, and we had no more than mounted our horses before we discovered that we were surrounded. We heard the tramp of cavalry on all sides. A quiet voice in the darkness made itself heard: "Don't shoot unless they resist!"

"Ride them down!" exclaimed Harry. My horse ran full into another horse, and he and his rider went down just as I used my pistol. Some one with an oath whacked me over the head with a sabre, my horse stumbled in the darkness, and down I went into chaos. I thought I heard someone singing, and then it seemed as if there was a free concert in progress, while I lay helpless in a great gully out of which I could not climb.

VIII

Making a great effort to climb from the gully into which I had fallen, my foot slipped, and I fell again, and continued to fall till I knew no more. When I came to life again I was not in a gully at all, but stretched out on a bed, with my boots on, and this fact fretted me to such an extent that I threw back the covering and rose to a sitting posture. My head was throbbing somewhat wildly, and I soon found that the cause of the pain was a towel that had been too tightly bound around my forehead. The towel changed into a bandage under my fingers, and I found that I could not compass the intricacies of the fastenings. I remembered that I had disposed safely of the papers I had found in the chair-arm. One was a passport signed by one of the biggest men in the country, authorizing Francis Leroy to pass in and out of the Union lines at any time, day or night, and the other—there were but two —was some useless information with respect to the movements of the Federal forces between Murfreesborough and Memphis.

As I came more and more to my senses, I knew that these papers had been the cause of my undoing; I could see in it, as plain as day, the hand of Jane Ryder, and I was truly sorry. I thought I had been around the world and back again, and I should have been very wise, but the bandage and Jane Ryder were too much for me. How did she know that I had secured the papers? And why did she permit the soldiers to attack me. I was feeling very foolish and childish.

Then I observed that a large man was sitting in front of the small fireplace, and his long legs were stretched completely across the hearth. His head was thrown back, his mouth was open, and he was sound asleep. There was half a handful of some kind of medicine in a saucer on the table, and I judged that the man would be better off for a dose of it. I suppose it was common table salt, but, whatever it was, the notion remained with me that it would be a help to the man. It was a fantastic notion, but it persisted, and finally I lifted the saucer, emptied the medicine in my palm, and transferred it to the open mouth of the man. It failed to arouse him; he merely closed his jaws on the dose and slept on.

I enjoyed the man's discomfiture before it occurred; I knew what a terrible splutter there would be when the stuff began to melt and run down his windpipe. I should have laughed aloud, but the bandage was hurting me terribly. With a vague hope of getting some relief from pain, I opened the door as softly as I could, went out and closed it behind me. Another door was open directly in front of me, and through this I went. In the room a woman was sitting at a window, her head in her hands. She looked up when she heard the slight noise I made, and I was surprised to find myself face to face with Jane Ryder. Her eyes were red and swollen with weeping, and her hands were all of a tremble.

"Will you please, ma'am, take this off?" I said, pointing to the bandage.

She placed her finger on her lip. "Sh-sh!" she whispered, and then, whipping around me, closed the door with no more noise than the wing of a night-bird might make. "In there, and don't move on your life."

She pointed to a closet, but I shook my head.

"Not if I can help myself," I said. "I have just come out of a deep, deep ditch, and I want to hear the splutter." I was whispering, too, such was the woman's influence. She looked at me in amazement; she tried to understand me; but she must have thought me out of my head, for her lips were twitching pitifully and her hands trembling. "It's the man in the next room," I whispered with a grin. "I put a handful of medicine in his mouth. Wait! you'll hear him directly."

"Oh, I am so sorry for you," she cried, wringing her hands. "I am as sorry for you as I am for myself."

"Then please take this bandage off and have my horse brought round."

"I can't! I can't! You're wounded. Go in the closet there."

"I'll go where you go, and I'll stay where you stay," I said; and I must have been talking too loud, for she placed her hand on my lips—and what should I do but hold it there and kiss it, the poor little trembling hand!

And then there came from the next room the famous splutter for which I had been waiting.

The soldier made a noise as if he were drowning. He gasped and coughed, and tried to catch his breath; he strangled and lost it, and, when he caught it again, made a sound as if he had a violent case of the whooping-cough. And all this time I was laughing silently, and I came near strangling myself.

Jane Ryder was far from laughter. She was as cool as a cucumber. With one quick movement, and with surprising strength, she had shoved me into the closet. Then she flung the door wide open. As she did so the guard cried out at the top of his voice that the prisoner had escaped. And if ever a man was berated it was that big soldier who had fallen asleep at the post of duty. "You drunken wretch!" she cried; "I knew how it would be; I knew it!" He tried to make an explanation, but she would not hear it. "Oh, I'll make you pay for this! Go—go and find him, and if you fail take your cut-throats away from here and never let me see them again. Report to my brother, and tell him how you carried out your orders. You were to take them all without a struggle, but you took only one, and you bring him here more dead than alive. He is wandering about in the woods now, out of his head."

"But he shot one of my men. Haven't you any feeling for the man that'll be cold and stiff by sun-up?"

"For the man, yes. You should have been the one to pay for your blundering. You failed to carry out your orders, and you had a dozen against three, and one of the three a negro."

The man started away, but his lagging footsteps showed that he had something on his mind, and in a few moments I heard him coming back. " 'Tain't no use to hunt for the man in the dark, and by sun-up his friends'll be buzzin' around here worse'n a nest of hornets. We are going back—going back," he repeated, "and you may report what you please."

Then the man went away, mumbling and mouthing to himself. As for me, I should have preferred to go with him. Pretty much everything is fair in war, and Jane Ryder was on the Union side. She knew of the ambuscade and had not told me; it was her duty not to tell. She would have made no sign if we had been going to our deaths. I have never felt more depressed in my life than I did at that moment. Something had slipped from under me, and I had nothing to stand on. I came out of the closet both angry and sorry. "I shall be obliged to you if you will find my hat," I said.

I tried hard to hide my real feelings, and with anyone else the effort would have been successful; but she knew. She came and stood by me and caught me by the arm. "Where would you go?" There was a baffled look in her eyes, and her voice was uneasy.

"Call your man," I said; "I will go with him; it is not his fault that he cannot find me; it is not his fault that I am hiding here in a woman's closet. Nor shall he be punished for it."

"Your hat is not here," she declared. "It must be where you fell. Do you know," she cried, "that you have killed a man? Do you know that?" Her tone was almost triumphant.

"Well, what of that?" I asked. "You set them on us, and the poor fellow took his chance with the rest. Gladly would I take his place." My head was hurting and I was horribly depressed.

She had turned away from me, but now she

flashed around with surprising quickness. "You are the cause of it all—yes, you! And, oh, if I could tell you how I hate you! If I could only show you what a contempt I have for you!" She was almost beside herself with anger, passion—I know not what. She shrank back from me, drew in a long breath, and fell upon the floor as if a gust of wind had blown her over; and then I began to have a dim conception of the power that moved and breathed in the personality of this woman. She fell, gave a long, shivering sigh, and, to all appearance, lay before me dead.

In an instant I was wild with remorse and grief. I seized a chair and sent it crashing into the hallway to attract attention. To this noise I added my voice, and yelled for help with lungs that had aroused the echoes on many a hunting-field. There were whisperings below, and apparently a hurried consultation, and then a young woman came mincing up the stairs. I must have presented a strange and terrifying spectacle with my head bandaged and my wild manner, for the woman, with a shriek, turned and ran down the stairs again. I cried again for someone to come to the aid of the lady, and presently someone

I was wild with remorse and grief

called up the stairs to know what the trouble was.

"Come and see," I cried. "The lady has fainted, and she may be dead."

I went into the room again, and, taking Jane Ryder in my arms, carried her into the next room and laid her on the bed. There was a pitcher of water handy, and I sprinkled her face and began to chafe her cold hands. After what seemed an age, the landlord came cautiously along the hall. "Call the woman," I commanded; "call the woman, and tell her to come in a hurry."

This he did, and then peeped in the room, taking care not to come inside the door. "What is the matter?" he said uneasily.

"Can't you see that the lady is ill?" I answered.

The woman—two women, indeed—came running in response to his summons. "Go in there and see what the trouble is. See if he has killed her. I told her he was dangerous. You shall pay for this," he said, shaking a threatening hand at me, though he came no farther than the door. "You think she has no friends and that you may use her as you please. But I tell you she has friends, and you will have to answer to them."

"Why talk like a fool?" said the elder of the

two women—the woman with whom I had talked in the inner room of the tavern. "You know as well as I do that this man has not hurt her. If it were some other man I'd believe you. She has only fainted."

"But fainting is something new to her. He has hurt her, and he shall pay for it," the man insisted.

"And I tell you," the woman repeated, "that he has not harmed a hair of her head. If he had do you think I'd be standing here denying it? Don't you know what I'd be doing?"

"If I am wrong I am quite ready to apologize. I was excited—was beside myself."

"I want none of your apologies," I said to the man. "I have a crow to pick with you, and I'll furnish a basket to hold the feathers."

"It is better to bear no malice," remarked the younger woman, calmly. "The Bible will tell you so."

"It is better to tell me the cause of the trouble," interrupted her elder.

"Why, I hardly know. I asked for my hat, and from one word to another we went till she flamed out at me, and said she hated me, and had a great contempt for me; and then she fell on the floor in a faint. I thought she was dead, but when I laid her on the bed there I saw her eyelids twitching.

The two women eyed each other in a way that displeased me greatly. "I told you so," said one. "It's the world's wonder," replied the other. And then Jane Ryder opened her eyes. It was natural that they should fall on me. She closed them again with a little shiver and then the natural color returned to her face. "I thought you were gone," she whispered.

"Did you think I would go and leave you like this? Do you really think I am a brute—that I have no feeling?" She closed her eyes again, as if reflecting.

"But I told you I hated you. Didn't you hear me? Couldn't you understand?"

"Perfectly," I replied. "I knew it before you told me; but, even so, could I go and leave you as you were just now? Consider, madam. Put yourself in my place—I who have never done you the slightest injury under the blue sky—" I was going on at I know not what rate, but she refused to listen.

"Oh, don't! don't! Oh, please go away!" she cried, holding her arms out toward me in supplicating fashion. It was an appeal not to be resisted, least of all by me. I looked at her—I gave her one glance, as the elderly woman took me by the arm.

"Come with me," she said; "you shall have a hat, though I hardly think it will fit you with the bandage round your head."

She led me downstairs, and, after some searching, she fished out a hat from an old closet, and it did as well as another. She asked me many questions as she searched. How long had I known the poor lady upstairs? and where did I meet her? She would have made a famous cross-questioner. I answered her with such frankness that she seemed to take a fancy to me.

"Some say that the poor lady upstairs is demented," she volunteered.

"Whoever says so lies," I replied. "She has more sense than nine-tenths of the people you meet."

"And then, again, some say she can mesmerize

folks." Then, seeing that the information failed to interest me, "What do you think of them—the mesmerizers?"

"I think nothing of them. If they could mesmerize me, I should like to see them do it."

"Oh, would you, you poor young man," she said, with a strange smile. "How would you know that you were mesmerized, and how would you help yourself?"

I know not what reply I made. A fit of dejection had seized me, and I could think of nothing but Jane Ryder. "You mustn't think of that young lady upstairs as hating you," said the woman, after she had brushed the hat and had asked me if I felt strong enough to walk a mile or more. "All she means is that she hates your principles. She hates secession, and she hates Secessionists. But something has upset her of late; she is not herself at all. I'm telling you the truth."

"She hates me; you may depend on that; but her hate makes no difference to me. I love her, and I'd love her if she were to cut my throat."

"Is that true? Are you honest? May I tell

her so some time—not now—but some time when you are far away?"

"To what end?" I asked. "She would tear her hair out if she knew it; she would never be happy again."

"You don't happen to love her well enough to join her side, do you?" This question was put hesitatingly, and, as I thought, with some shy hope that it would receive consideration.

"Madam, you have tried to be kind to me in your way, and therefore I will say nothing to wound your feelings; but if a man were to ask me that question he would receive an answer that would prevent him from repeating it in this world."

"Humpty-dumpty jumped over the wall!" exclaimed the woman with a laugh. "I knew what you'd say, but I had my reasons for asking the question; you must go now; and bear in mind," she went on with a sudden display of feeling, "that the war has made such devil's hags of the women, and such devil's imps of the men, that everything is in a tangle. You'll know where you are when you go in the next room. And you must forgive me. I am Jane Ryder's mother."

And, sure enough, I was in the tavern in the woods, and sitting by the hearth was Whistling Jim. To say that he was glad to see me would hardly describe the outward manifestation of his feelings. Someone in the camp, he didn't know who, had sent him word that he'd find me at this house, and he had been waiting for more than an hour, the last half of it with many misgivings. He and Harry had escaped without any trouble, and my horse had followed them so closely that they thought I was on his back. But when they saw that he was riderless, they thought that I had either been captured or killed. Once at camp, Harry Herndon drummed up as many of the Independents as would volunteer, and they had gone in search of me; Whistling Jim heard them riding along the road as he was coming to the tavern.

The faithful negro had a hundred questions to ask, but I answered him in my own way. I was determined that none but those directly concerned should ever know that I had been held a prisoner or that Miss Ryder had a hand in the night's work; and I wished a thousand times over that I had not known it myself. The old saying, worn to a frazzle with repetition, came to me with new force, and I was sadly alive to the fact that where ignorance is bliss 'tis folly to be wise.

The night was now far advanced, and once at my quarters I flung myself on the rude bed that had been provided for me, and all the troubles and tangles in this world dissolved and disappeared in dreamless slumber. When morning broke I felt better. My head was sore, but the surgeon removed the bandage, clipped the hair about the wound, took a stitch or two that hurt worse than the original blow, and in an hour I had forgotten the sabre-cut.

Singular uneasiness pervaded my thoughts. More than once I caught myself standing still as if expecting to hear something. I tried in vain to shake off the feeling, and at last I pretended to trace it to feverishness resulting from the wound in the scalp; but I knew this was not so—I knew that one of the great things of life was behind it all; I knew that I had come to the hour that young men hope for and older men dread; I knew that for good or evil my future was wrapped in the mystery and tangle of which Jane Ryder was the centre. My common-sense tried to picture her forth as the spider waiting in the centre of her web for victims, but my heart resented this and told me that she herself had been caught in the web and found it impossible to get away.

I wandered about the camp and through the town with a convalescent's certificate in my pocket and the desperation of a lover in my heart; and at the very last, when night was falling, it was Jasper Goodrum, of the Independents, who gave me the news I had been looking for all day.

"You'd better pick up and go with us, Shannon; our company is going to raid the tavern to-night, and to-morrow we take the road. Oh, you are not hurt bad," he said, trying to interpret the expression on my face; "you can go, and I think I can promise you a little fun. They say a spy is housed there, and we propose to smoke him out to-night. Get your horse; we start in half an hour."

He went off down the street, leaving me staring at him open-mouthed. When he was out of sight I turned and ran toward the camp as if my life depended on it.

IX

I knew no more what I intended to do than the babe unborn. What I did know was that Jane Ryder was in that house, in all probability; and that fact stung me. She had aided me to escape, even though she had had a hand in my capture, and I felt that the least I could do would be to take her away from there, willingly if she could come, forcibly if she hesitated.

On the way to the camp I met Whistling Jim, and he stopped me. He was astride his horse and leading mine. "Dey er gwine on a ride now terreckly, Marse Cally, an' I 'lowed maybe you'd want ter go 'long wid um."

For answer I swung myself on my horse and, bidding the negro to follow if he desired, put spurs to the sorrel and went flying in the direction of the tavern. I did not turn my head to see whether Whistling Jim was following, but rode straight ahead. It strikes me as curious, even yet, that the darkness should have fallen so suddenly on that particular day. When Goodrum spoke to me I supposed that the sun was still shining; when I turned into the road that led to the house it was dark. I reached the place in the course of a quarter of an hour, and as I leaped from my horse I heard the negro coming close behind me. I waited for him to come up and dismount, and then I bade him knock at the door, and when it was opened I told him to stand by the horses.

The door was opened by the woman who had spoken so kindly with me. "You here again?" she cried with an air of surprise. "You would make it very hard for her if she were here, but I think she is gone. You'll not see her again, my dear, and I, for one, am glad of it. There's no one here but myself and my son."

"Your son is the one I want," I replied. "Tell him to come at once. I have news for him." The woman had no need to call him, however, for the inner door opened as I spoke, and out came Jane Ryder in the garb of a man—cloak, boots, and all.

I had an idea that she would shrink from me

or show some perturbation; but I was never more
mistaken in my life. In a perfectly easy and
natural manner—the manner of a young man—
she came up and held out her hand. "I think
this is Mr. Shannon; Miss Ryder told me your
name. I have to thank you for some recent
kindness to her."

I shook her hand very cordially, saying that
nothing I could do for Miss Ryder would be
amiss. "As it happens," I went on, "I can do
something for you now. Will you come with
me?"

For one fleeting moment her woman's hesitation held her, and then her woman's curiosity pre-
vailed. "With pleasure," she said.

As we started for the door the woman interfered. "I wouldn't go with him," she declared
with some bluntness. "You don't have to go and
you sha'n't. You don't know what he's up to."

This failed to have the effect I feared it would.
"Don't you suppose I can take care of myself,
mother?"

"I know what I know," replied the woman, sullenly, "and it wouldn't take much to make me
tell it."

"Then, for heaven's sake, say what you have to say and be done with it," I exclaimed. "Only a very few minutes lie between this person and safety. If you have anything to tell out with it."

"Your blue eyes and baby face fooled me once, but they'll not fool me again. You know more than you pretend to know," said the woman.

"I know this: if this person remains here ten minutes longer he will regret it all the days of his life. Now, trust me or not, just as you please. If he is afraid to come with me let him say so, and I will bid him farewell forever and all who are connected with him. Do you trust me?" I turned to Jane Ryder and held out my hand.

"I do," she replied. She came nearer, but did not take my hand.

"Then, in God's name, come with me!" I cried. She obeyed my gesture and started for the door.

"Where are you going?" wailed the mother. "Tell me—tell me!"

I was sorry for her, but I made her no answer.

I anticipated this scene as little as I did the fact that Jane Ryder would come with me. I was prepared to carry her off if she refused, but

I was ill prepared for the rumpus that this quiet-looking woman kicked up. She followed us to the door and stood wailing while I tried to persuade Jane Ryder to mount my horse. She hesitated, but I fairly lifted her into the saddle. The stirrup-straps were too short, but that made no difference. I sprang on the horse behind her, and, reaching forward, seized the reins and turned the horse's head in a direction that would bring us into the town by a detour, so that we should miss the Independents, who would follow the road that I had followed in coming.

"Where are you taking me?" inquired Jane Ryder.

"To safety," I replied. "The house is to be raided to-night, and I decided to bring you away. You saved me from a prison, and now I propose to save you."

"I saved you? You are mistaken; it was that foolish woman, Miss Ryder."

"Well, she said that you are her dearest friend, and I'm saving you to please her."

"You needn't hold me so tight. I'm in no danger of falling off. Where are you taking me?"

"If hate could kill you, you would fall dead from this
horse"

"To General Forrest." She caught her breath, and then did her utmost to fling herself from the horse. When she found that her strength was not equal to the task of removing my arms or lifting them so she could slip from the saddle, she began to use her tongue, which has ever been woman's safest weapon.

"You traitor!" she cried; "oh, you traitor! I wish I had died before I ever saw you."

"But this is the safest course," I insisted. "You will see, and then you will thank me for bringing you away."

"And I thought you were a gentleman; I took you for an honest man. Oh, if hate could kill you you would fall dead from this horse. What have I done that I should come in contact with such a villain?"

"You have a pistol," I said—I had felt it against my arm—"and it is easy for you to use it. If you think so meanly of me why not rid the earth of such a villain?"

"Do you know who I am?" she asked with a gasp of apprehension.

"Why, certainly," I answered. "Do you think I'd be taking the trouble to save you else?"

"Trouble to save me? Save me? Why, I hope your savage General will hang me as high as Haman."

"He would if he were a savage," I said, "and he would if you were a man. And he may put you in prison as it is; you would certainly go there if captured by the Forty Thieves. I am taking one chance in a thousand. But better for you to be in prison, where you will be safe, than for you to be going around here masquerading as a man and subjecting yourself to the insults of all sorts of men."

"You are the only man that has ever insulted me. Do you hear? You—gentleman!" she hissed. "Can't you see that I despise you? Won't you believe it? Does it make no difference?"

"Not the least in the world," I replied. "Now, you must compose yourself; you can be brave enough when you will—I think you are the bravest woman I ever saw——"

"I wish I could say you are a brave man; but you are an arrant coward: you, the soldier that plans to capture women."

"You must compose yourself," I repeated.

"In a few minutes we shall be in the presence of General Forrest, and I should like to see you as calm as possible. I don't know, but I think you will be safe. It was our only chance." The nearer we drew to headquarters the more my anxiety rose; yes, and my sympathy. "By the living Lord," I cried, "you *shall* be safe!"

"Noble gentleman! to entrap a woman and then declare she shall not be entrapped! To gain whatever honor there may be in a woman's capture by running ahead of his ruffians and capturing her himself! This is Southern manliness— this is Southern chivalry! I am glad I know it for what it really is. Do you know," she went on, "that I really thought—that—I—I— You are the first man I was ever deceived in—I—"

"Come now," said I, not unmoved, for my feelings ran far ahead of hers and I knew what she would say and how hurt she was; "come now, you must be calm. Everything depends on that —everything."

Near General Forrest's headquarters I dismounted and walked by the side of my horse. Then when Whistling Jim came up, and I would have helped her from the saddle, "Don't touch me!" she exclaimed. She jumped from the saddle to the ground and stood before me, and for the first time I was ashamed and afraid. "This way," I said. Then to the guard at the door, "Private Shannon, of Captain Forrest's company, to see the General."

"He's right in there," said the guard with good-natured informality. I rapped at the inner door, and heard the well-known voice of General Forrest bidding me to enter.

I saluted, and he made some motion with his hand, but his eye wandered over me and rested on my companion. Then, after a moment, they returned to me. "What's the matter, Shannon?"

"I have brought to you here one who came to my rescue last night when I had been captured by a scouting party. We had gone to see the young fellow who, you will remember, was wounded in our last affair at the river—you saw him in the cabin. He was carried away the next day by his friends, but grew so ill that he could be taken no farther than the house on the turnpike two miles from town."

"You didn't let 'em git you just dry so, did

you?" he asked. And then I gave him the details of the affair from beginning to end. "I thought Herndon was mighty keen to go," he remarked with a laugh. "You say this young fellow fixed it so you could git away? And then you went back and captured him? That don't look fair, does it?" He regarded me with serious countenance.

"It is a lady, General, and I did not want her to fall in rough hands." He uttered an exclamation of impatience and surprise, and made an indignant gesture. "Now, look here, Shannon, that is a matter that I won't tolerate. I've a great mind to—" He paused, hearing the voice of his wife, who was visiting him. "Go back in there and tell Mrs. Forrest to come in here a minute, and do you stay out till I call you. I'm going to look into this business, and if it ain't perfectly square all the way through you'll pay for it."

I hunted for Mrs. Forrest, hat in hand, and soon found her. I must have had a queer expression on my face, for she observed it. "You must be frightened," she said.

"I am, madam, for another as well as myself,"

and then I told her, as we walked along very slowly, just how the matter lay. She regarded me very seriously for a moment, and then smiled. She was a handsome lady, and this smile of hers, full of promise as it was, made her face the most beautiful I have ever seen before or since. It is a large saying, but it is true.

I remember that I remained in the corridor cooling my heels a weary time, but finally Mrs. Forrest came out. "You may go in now," she said. "It is all right; I'm glad I was called; I think I have made the General understand everything as I do. There are some things that men do not understand as well as women, and it is just as well that they do not. I am sure you will be very kind to that little woman in there."

I tried to thank her, but there is a gratitude that cannot be expressed in words, and I could but stand before her mumbling with my head bent. "I know what you would say," she remarked, graciously. "The General and I have perfect confidence in you."

I went into the room where General Forrest and Jane Ryder were. "Shannon, what are you and Herndon up to? What do you mean by going on in this way?" He spoke with some severity, but there was a humorous twinkle in his blue-gray eyes. "More than that, you took occasion to prejudice the jury. What did you say to Mrs. Forrest?"

"I simply asked her to be kind to the lady in here."

"Well, she was all of that," said the General, "and she threatened me with her displeasure if I wasn't kind to you, and as she's the only human being that I'm really afeared of, I reckon I'll have to let you off this time. Oh, you needn't look so smiling; you are to be punished, and that heavily. You are to be responsible for this young woman. You are to take charge of her and restore her to her own people—mind you, to her own people. You are responsible to me, and I reckon you know what that means; if you don't you can just ask somebody that knows me."

I knew what it meant well enough, and I knew what his words meant. "The lady is as safe with me, General, as if she were in her mother's arms."

"Now, that's the way to talk, and I believe you," said General Forrest.

All this time Jane Ryder had said not a word. She sat very quietly, but there was not a sign of gloom or dejection in her face. But uneasiness looked from her eyes. She spoke presently, while General Forrest was looking through a large morocco memorandum-book that was a little the worse for wear. "If you please," she said, "I should like to go back to my friends tonight, if they are not all killed. They can do you no harm even if they are alive. They are only a couple of women."

"Well, they are not killed," replied General Forrest without looking up. "Wimmen make war on me and do a lot of damage, but I don't make war on them. I'm letting you off on a technicality, Miss Ryder. You are not a spy; you have never been inside my lines until tonight; and yet you were in a fair way to find out a good many things that the other side would like to know."

"I never found out as much as I'd like to know," she replied; "and since he came bothering me I haven't found out anything."

Apparently General Forrest ignored the remark. He turned to me with a slip of paper in his hand. "You'll have to change your name, Shannon. This passport is made out to someone else. Read it."

He handed it to me, and I read aloud: "The bearer of this, Captain Francis Leroy, is authorized to pass in and out the Federal lines, night or day, without let or hindrance." It was signed by a great man at Washington and countersigned by one almost as great.

"Why, that belongs to me," said Jane Ryder; "where did you find it?"

"I reckon it's just a duplicate," said the General, smiling. "I've had it some time."

A little frown of perplexity appeared above Jane Ryder's eyes, and if it had never gone away until she solved the mystery of this passport it would have been there yet, for neither one of us ever knew where General Forrest obtained the precious document.

"You will want to go out of my lines, Shannon, and you'll want to come back, so I'll fix it up for you." He went into the next room and dictated to an orderly, and presently brought me a paper signed with his own name, and I have it yet.

Everything was ready for us to take our leave, and we did so. "You are a different man from what I thought you," said Jane Ryder to General Forrest, "and I have to thank you for your kindness and consideration."

"It ain't what people think of you—it's what you are that counts," replied General Forrest. I have thought of this homely saying hundreds of times, and it rings truer every time I repeat it to myself. It covers the whole ground of conscience and morals.

As I was going out, Jane Ryder being in advance, the General said to me again, "Don't make no mistake about what I mean. You are responsible to me for the safety of that young lady. I believe in you, but I may be wrong. If I am wrong you'd just as well go out and hang yourself and save me the trouble."

"You needn't worry about me, General. I can take care of myself," declared Jane Ryder. We went out of the house and came to where Whistling Jim was holding the horses. I dismissed him then and there, and told him to put his horse in the stable and have plenty of feed for mine. But Jane Ryder, for reasons of her

own, preferred to walk, so that Whistling Jim
went away with the two horses and we were left
to ourselves.

I remember that I said very little during that
long walk, and all the burden of the conversation
fell on the young woman. She was not at all
elated over the narrow escape she had had, and
preferred to make light of it, but I knew that,
under different circumstances, she would have
been put in prison in Richmond, and I think that
her nature would have succumbed to close con-
finement.

"You have had your way, after all, but I am
not sure that I like it," she said. She waited for
me to make some reply, but none was forthcom-
ing. "I hope you don't think you have won a
great victory. If I had been a man, perhaps the
victory would have been the other way."

"I didn't compel you to come with me," I remarked.

"You mean I came of my own accord. If I
did, it was to avoid a scene before my mother—
the lady you saw at the house. I didn't want her
to hear you bluster and threaten; and, besides, I
wanted to tell you what I think of you. We

have both had our way. My mother thinks you are a gentleman in a way, and I know what I know."

I trudged along by her side silently; I had no relish for an argument in which I was sure to get the worst of it. In some matters a man is no match for a woman: he cannot cope with her in a war of words. Nor will silence discomfit them. At least, it had no such effect in this instance, for the more I was silent, the louder and faster she talked, and, apparently, the angrier she became.

"You will boast, no doubt," said she, "and tell your comrades how you lorded it over a young fellow who turned out to be a woman—how you compelled her to go with you to General Forrest's headquarters. But how did you know me? How did you know who I was?"

I laughed aloud. "Why, I'd know you through a thousand disguises, as I knew you here that first night."

"I don't believe it; you didn't know me that first night; you had never seen me but once before, and you couldn't have known me. How did you know me to-night? You won't answer, or if you do you'll say you knew me by my swagger. Anything to insult a woman. I'd like to be a man for a few hours just to see how they feel toward women—just how much more contempt they feel than they show. I tell you, you didn't know me that first night."

"Then why did I insist on going home with you?"

This rather stumped her. "Because—because you thought I was a slip of a lad, and you knew you could impose on me. If you had known I was a woman, you wouldn't have called me a little devil— Yes, you would!" she quickly added. "You would have abused me worse than that if you had known I was a woman. How did you know—if you knew?"

"By your eyes; the moment I looked into them fairly I said to myself, 'Here's Jane Ryder again; no one has eyes like hers!' "

She was silent for a little space, and then, "Did it never occur to you that it would be politer to refer to me as *Miss* Jane Ryder?" Now, I had never thought of her as Miss Jane Ryder, and I told her so. "Are my eyes so peculiar that you would know them anywhere? Are they positively hideous, as the young women say?" I hesitated, and she went on, "But why do I ask? No matter what you think, it can never, never make any difference to me, after the way you have treated me to-night, and I hope that when you bid me good-by, as you will have to do directly, that I shall never see you again."

"That is the talk of a child, and you are supposed to be a grown woman," I replied. "You know very well that I am obliged to carry out the orders of my General, no matter how much they go against the grain."

She stopped in the road and tried to read my face even in the dark. "Do you really mean that?" and then, without waiting for an answer, she turned and ran, and I followed the best I could.

X

It soon dawned on me that this surprising young woman was as nimble with her feet as a schoolboy. She scampered away from me in a way to put me on my mettle, and she must have run nearly half a mile before I could come up with her. I touched her on the shoulder lightly, crying "Caught!"

"There is no getting rid of you," she answered.

"Oh, but there is, as you will discover," I said. "Once with your kin-people, you will see no more of me." I was vexed, but my ill-humor seemed to add to her high spirits, and she talked away quite blithely. When we came to the door it was open, and the mother, who had been kind to me, stood there waiting. She was crying and wringing her hands, and, for a moment, I thought she had been maltreated by those whose duty it was to raid the house. But her trouble was of quite another kind.

"What have you done with her?" she asked.

"She is here with me," I replied. But when I turned to confirm my words, Jane Ryder had disappeared. I could only stare at the woman blankly and protest that she had been at my side a moment ago before. "I knew it!" wailed the woman. "First comes you to wheedle her away, and then come your companions to search the house for her. I knew how it would be. I never knew but one man you could trust with a woman, and he was so palsied that a child could push him over. And the little fool was fond of you, too." And with that she wailed louder than ever.

"But, my good woman—" I began.

"Don't good woman me!" she cried. "You don't look like that kind of a man, but I knew it; I knew how it would be!"

"Fiddlesticks and frog's eggs!" I cried. "Stop your crying. She is here somewhere. You know well enough that I wouldn't have returned without her. She came to the door with me. I'd have you to know, madam, that I'm not the man you take me for. Do you think I'd injure a hair of her head? It is you that have injured her by allowing her to masquerade as a man—a little thing like that, with nobody to advise her. You are her mother and pretend to be fond of her; why didn't you advise her against all this? Why didn't you take a hickory to her and compel her to remember her sex? You are the cause of it all —yes, you!"

I spoke in a very loud tone, for I was very angry, and I knew that the only way to contend with a woman was to make more noise than she could. Just as I was about to continue my railing protest, Jane Ryder came through an inner door, dressed, as she should be, in the garb of her sex. Her toilette would have been complete but for the fact that in her haste her hair had fallen loose from its fastenings and now flowed over her shoulders and down to her waist, black as night and as shiny as silk.

"I thank you both for your good opinions," she said, making a mock courtesy, "especially the chivalrous Mr. Carroll Shannon, with his straps, and his hickories, and his riding-whips, and I hope he will soon get a woman on whom he can use them all."

"Oh, Jane! Jane!" cried the other, "why will

you worry those who love you? Why will you try them so?"

The young woman's face fell at that, and she seemed to be very contrite. She went quickly across the room and never paused until she found herself in the woman's arms, and showed her love by so many quaint and delicate little caresses, and had such a dainty and bewitching way about her, that no human could have held out against her. The woman's face had cleared on the instant and was no more clouded with grief and anxiety. "You see how she is," said the woman to me; "hurting you to the heart one minute and making you forget it the next."

"I see," I replied; "but you should control her. You should make her remember who and what she is, and not permit her to go about as a man or boy. Don't you know how dangerous it is?"

"Oh, but she's her own mistress," the woman explained. "She can wheedle, and no one can say her nay. But I'm glad she went away to-night, though I was terribly afraid for her. She had no more than got out of hearing before there came a pack of troopers, and nothing must do but they must search the whole house from top to bottom. They were hunting for Leroy, too, and if she had been here there would have been trouble."

"What did I tell you?" I exclaimed. "I captured her ahead of them, carried her to General Forrest, and now she is my prisoner. I am responsible for her."

"I believe I had rather the others had captured me," Jane Ryder declared. The woman looked at me and shook her head, as much as to say, "Never believe her."

"Why did you trouble yourself?" Jane Ryder inquired. "I am sure I never gave you any cause to worry yourself about me. If you think you have done me a service you were never more mistaken in your life. You have simply destroyed my usefulness for the time being; but you have given me an opportunity to show you what I think of your intermeddling."

"Jane! you know that he has meddled with you only for your own good," said the older woman. "You ought to thank him on your knees."

"On my knees!" she exclaimed angrily. "On my knees! I dare say he would like to see me on my knees before him, but he'll see me dead first." I was surprised at the heat she showed over the matter.

"Your mother," I said, "has simply used an unfortunate expression. You owe me nothing —and if you owed me everything a kind word would more than repay me."

She bit her lip, but made no reply. "It's her way," explained the mother, "and I'm free to say it's a very poor way. It has always been her way. Love her and she'll hurt you; do her a favor and she'll pretend to despise you. Her kind words are as scarce as pearls among the poor. Scarce, but when they are spoken they make up for all the rest. Don't be angry with her; a big man like you shouldn't care what a child like her says."

"Child! I am older than he is," said Jane Ryder.

"But age is not age unless it has experience and judgment," remarked the older woman, serenely. "Without them, age is another form of childishness."

"What are you going to do with me?" asked Jane Ryder, turning to me. She was evidently weary of a discussion of which she was the subject.

She had placed her finger squarely on my perplexity, for this was indeed the great problem that I had to solve—what should I do with her? Not to-morrow, nor the day after, but now—to-night. The question had occurred to me a dozen times, but I had put it aside, trusting its solution to the moment when it could be no longer postponed. I hesitated so long that both of the women sat staring at me. "You have not answered my question," said Jane Ryder, "and it is important that I should know."

"I might give you your parole for the night," I answered.

"You persist in regarding me as your prisoner?"

"I have my orders," I replied. "You know that as well as I do."

"Thank you for your information. Goodnight!" and she was gone before I could say a word, even if I had known what to say. All I could do was to stare blankly at the door through which she had disappeared. I had known all along that if she once took the matter in her own hands I should be powerless, for she was a woman —and such a woman! I could no more hold her prisoner against her will than I could fly.   My whole nature revolted at the thought of it.   She was a woman—a dangerous woman, no doubt, but still a woman—and that settled it for me.

And then, after I had looked at the door long enough to stare it out of countenance, if it had had one, I turned to the mother and stared at her. There was just the shadow of a smile hovering around her lips, and it nettled me.   "She is parading as a man," I said, "and I think I shall treat her as one.   A man can be rapped on the head, tied up, and bundled about, without regard for his comfort."

"And yet," said the mother, with her knowing smile, "you wouldn't hurt a hair of her head, nor give her a moment's discomfort."   She made the statement with so much complacency that I was more than irritated; I was vexed.

"If you knew me," I declared, "you wouldn't say that.   I have no patience with women who try to play the man."

"I know you well enough to say what I have said," she replied.   "You have a face that tells no lies—and more's the pity."

"Where has she gone?" I inquired.

"That I can't tell you," the mother replied; "but it would be the wonder of the world if she had gone to bed. We who love her have no power to control her. She needs a stronger hand than ours."

"I could tell you something if I would," she remarked presently; "but it would be like feeling my way in the dark, and I dare not. Yet there is another thing I will tell you that can do no harm, though I promised to keep it to myself. If you stay here you will get in trouble. The man you shot night before last has a brother, and this brother is determined to capture you. I'm telling you this because I think you are a good young man. I had a son once who, if he had lived, should be about your age, and I would have thanked any woman in the world to have given him the warning I have given you. You can gain nothing by remaining here. You can return in the morning. Jane will be here; she is not going to run away from you."

"Nevertheless, I must do my duty," I said. "With your permission, I shall remain here. Does Jane Ryder know of the purpose of this fellow?"

"Oh, no; I wouldn't tell her. She has trouble enough." She paused and hesitated. "Why not go? There is the door; it is unlocked and you will still have time to join your friends. This is all I can say to you—all I can do for you."

"No; you can pray for me. And another thing: if you hear any noise cover up your head and make Jane Ryder cover hers."

"I'm sure I don't know what to make of you," she said, puckering her forehead as she stood in the door.

"But I think I know what to make of you and your daughter," I replied, with a laugh.

"Above all things, don't misjudge us," and with that she was gone, closing the door behind her.

How long I sat there I know not; it may have been one hour or it may have been many; but some time during the night there came a rap at the door and the pictures of Jane Ryder were blotted out of the fire and went flitting up the chimney. The knocking was on the outer door, which was unlocked, as the woman had said, and I cried out, "Come in!" Responsive to the invitation, Whistling Jim made his appearance, and

I was more than glad to see him. I discovered for the first time that I had been oppressed by my loneliness, for my spirits rose to a great height.

He seemed very glad to see me, for he laughed aloud. "I bet a dollar you ain't had no supper," he said, "an' I tuck an' brung you some. 'Tain't much, but it's better'n none." But I had no appetite. "I'm mighty glad I brung yo' pistols, too, kaze dey's sump'n wrong gwine on 'roun' here. I seed two er th'ee men prowlin' roun' in de bushes ez I come 'long. Marse Cally, how come you ter leave yo' pistols in yo' saddle? You ain't been a-doin' dataway. I speck dat ar little man you had up in front er you had sump'n ter do wid it." He laughed, but I found nothing humorous in the allusion. "Did I say 'oman, Marse Cally?" I shook my head. "Kaze ef I did, it slipped out des dry so. I wuz comin' atter you anyhow, but Marse Harry holla'd at me an' tol' me fer ter fin' you an' say dat de troops gwineter move in de mornin' an' our comp'ny starts fust."

I nibbled the food he had brought me, with some particularly heavy thoughts in regard to the

course we were to take. Yesterday I was a boy,
and a very foolish one, but to-day I felt myself
to be a man. The feeling was the growth of a
night, but it gave me new confidence in myself,
and, coupled with it, an assurance that I had
never had before, and that has remained with me
all through the long years that have intervened.
I think it must have caught the eye of Whistling
Jim—the change, I mean—for he regarded me
curiously and closely.

"Marse Cally," he said after a while, "I b'lieve
you done got mo' settled, sence—dog ef I don't
b'lieve dat it's been sence yistiddy! I dunner
wharbouts de change is, but it sho' is dar. It
mought be de way you look at me, an' it mought
be de way you don't look at me—an' ef you ain't
done grow'd bigger I ain't no nigger."

"I have only ceased to be giddy for the time
being," I said. "I am afraid I have some serious work cut out for me to-night. If you want
to go you are welcome to do so, and if you stay
I'll be glad to have you. I don't know anyone I
had rather have near me when a row springs up."

"Me, Marse Cally? You sholy don't mean
me." It was plain that he was delighted. "You

know how skeery I is, Marse Cally, when dey's a row gwine on. I can't he'p gittin' skeer'd ter save my life. But it's de same way 'bout leavin' you; I'm skeer'd ter leave you. I couldn't go out dat door fer ter save my life." Whistling Jim held out his long, slim hands where he could look at them. Then he ran the scale of an imaginary piano, once, twice, and shivered again. "I tell you, Marse Cally, I'm a-gittin' skeerder an' skeerder. I wish dey'd come on ef dey comin'."

"Well," said I, "I'll place the key of the door on the mantel here, and you can go out whenever you want to."

But he protested almost violently. "Don't you dast ter do dat, Marse Cally! You put dat key in yo' pocket, an' let it stay dar." Nevertheless, I laid it on the mantel. The negro looked at it more than once, and finally, as if taking leave of the temptation it represented, blew it a kiss from his long fingers.

As he sat down, four men filed into the room through the inner door, which had opened almost noiselessly.

XI

The men came in treading on one another's heels. The leader was a thick-set, heavily built fellow, and he had an evil-looking eye. He was evidently a soldier, or had been one, for he had the air and bearing that is unmistakable in a man who has seen service. He had a heavy jaw, and I noticed that his hair was cropped close to his head. The others appeared to be civilians, plain honest men, but ready, as were many men in Tennessee in those days, to help the Union cause in a quiet way.

"You said thar was only one," remarked one of them to the short-haired man.

"I only told you what Captain Leroy said," replied the leader.

"Well, you better had 'a' fetched Leroy along," commented the man, and I judged that he had small stomach for the work before him.

I realized that the time had come for me to

The leader . . . had an evil-looking eye

speak up. "State your business," said I. "What do you want with me?"

"We want you to go with us," replied the short-haired man; "and we'll get our wants, too."

"Where am I to go?"

"You'll know when you get there," was the answer.

"By which road?" I asked. "I am very careful about the roads I travel."

"We'll look after the roads all right," he replied. "Will you go peaceable or not?"

"Just for the looks of the thing," I replied, "I'd rather have it said that I surrendered only after a struggle." Glancing at the three men the ruffian had brought with him, I was confirmed in my impression that the affair was by no means to their taste. If they had made a rush all together it would have been the easiest matter in the world to overpower me, but somehow they hung back.

"Come on," the man cried to his companions, making as if he would lead them. They hesitated, and it was then that I gave them my views of the situation.

"Gentlemen," I said, "I take you for honest, fair-minded men, and I would advise you to have no hand in this business. This man's orders are from no competent authority, and I give you fair warning that you will bitterly regret your part in this night's work if you live through it."

I could see anxiety, not fear, creep into their faces, and a wholesome doubt of their leader's good faith. I was satisfied that my words had taken the edge off their eagerness, and this was all I hoped to do. I think the ruffian must have felt that his companions were weakening, for he paused and turned toward them, with his hand under his coat, as if in the act of drawing a weapon. What he intended to say I never knew, for, as he turned toward them, still watching me out of the corner of his evil eye, Whistling Jim was upon him.

Seizing the man in his arms, he whirled him around until he could get sufficient impetus, and then threw him against the wall as if he had been fired from a catapult. If you have never witnessed the fury of genuine fright it is to be hoped you never will, for there is something hideous about it. The ruffian had hardly hit the wall before the negro was upon him again, making a noise in his throat like some wild animal, his face distorted and the muscles of his arms and body standing out as prominently as if he were covered with huge wens or tumors.

The man had not been so badly stunned by his collision with the wall but that he could turn over, and by the time the negro reached him he had drawn his pistol half-way from his pocket; but that was all. Whistling Jim seized the hand and held it, and, using his head as a battering-ram, jammed it into the man's stomach and into his face. Then he dragged the limp body toward the fireplace, crying, "Git out de way, Marse Cally. I'm gwine ter put 'im whar he can't pester nobody else. Ef I don't he sho will shoot me, kaze I done seed his pistol."

While the negro was thus engaged with the most dangerous of the men, it is not to be supposed that I was idle. The three companions of the ruffian started to his aid when Whistling Jim began operations—their hesitation suddenly turning into indignation when they beheld the spectacle of a negro assaulting a white man. The foremost went down under the chair with which I struck him, the second one tripped over the fallen body and also went down with my assistance. The third man suddenly found the frame of the well-made chair fitting around his neck like the yoke of an ox. I did my best to pull his head off in order to recover my weapon, but his neck was tougher than the joints of white oak, and the two long legs that went to make up the back of the chair came off in my hand, thus giving me a bludgeon very much to my taste.

It was at this juncture that the negro came dragging the body of the ruffian and declaring his intention of giving him a foretaste of torment. My anger was of such a blind and unreasoning sort that I had no objections to the horrible proceeding, and if there had been no sudden diversion I should, in all probability, have aided him in carrying out his purpose. But there came a tremendous knocking at the door, and I could hear someone rapping and kicking at the panels trying to force an entrance. So I laid a restraining hand on the negro and bade him drop the almost lifeless body.

Giving him one of the chair-legs, and bidding him keep an eye on the three men, who evidently had had enough of the rough things of life, I went to the door.   The key was in a position to reflect the light, and I had the door open in a moment; but whoever had rapped to get in seemed to have changed his mind.   No one came in and no one made an effort to enter, but in another moment I heard the voice of Jane Ryder. "Run! run!" she cried.   "Run, if you want to escape!   The back yard is full of Union soldiers!"

But I thought that this was only a ruse on the part of the little lady to get rid of me, and, instead of getting away, as I should have done, I stepped out into the hallway.   The sight that I saw filled me with indignation, for there stood Jane Ryder, leaning against her mother, and rigged out in the toggery of a man.

I took her by the arm, and I must have gripped it roughly, for she winced.   "If you know what is good for you," I said, very sternly, "you will get yourself out of this wretched garb and throw it in the fire.   Will you go?"

"How can I go when you are holding me?" she

asked piteously. I released her and she went up the stairway sobbing.

Half-way up the stairs, she turned to me. "You will be sorry you didn't go when I told you. You couldn't go now if you wanted to," and with that she disappeared.

I could have cracked my silly pate at the sight of her weeping. I felt a hand on my arm, and found her mother standing at my side, laughing softly. Seeing that I regarded her with unfeigned astonishment, she laughed the louder. "You are the first that has ever mastered her. She is beyond me. When I married my second husband she declared that I had sold my interest in her for a pair of side-whiskers."

The mother said this so pathetically that I could but laugh, seeing that there was so much incongruity between the remark and the situation all about us. My laughter must have jarred her, for she said with some asperity, "You are laughing now, but in a minute you will be laughing on the other side of your mouth!"

And it was even as she said. A file of soldiers entered from the rear, and before I had time to move or raise a hand they had me surrounded.

Their leader was a man full of laughter and good-humor. "Consider yourself a prisoner," he said to me. "How are you, mother? You are looking well. Where is sister? Upstairs? Well, get her down, for we must be moving away from here. What is all this?" He looked into the room out of which I had come, and saw there the evidences of a struggle, as well as the victims thereof.

He bustled about with an alertness that seemed to be prepared for anything that might happen. I saw at once that he was a West Pointer. I had seen not more than a dozen graduates of the great military academy, but enough to recognize the characteristics that marked them all. These characteristics are wellnigh indescribable, but they are all included in the terms "soldier and gentleman."

"The bruiser has been bruised," he laughed. "You are looking well, mother; keep it up for the sake of the children. Tell sister to hurry up; we are in a tight place here."

As he spoke, there was the noise of another scuffle in the room. I turned just in time to see Whistling Jim fling himself upon the man, who had risen to a sitting position and was making an effort to draw his pistol. The negro wrenched the weapon from him, threw it out of reach, seized the hand that had held it and crunched it between his teeth with such savage ferocity that the ruffian howled with pain.

"Oh, come!" cried the officer. "This won't do, you know; this won't do at all. I won't put up with it."

"Ef I hadn't er ketched him when I did he'd er shot me daid," Whistling Jim explained; "me er Marse Cally one. You don't know dat man, suh. He been follerin' atter we-all fer de longest."

"I know him well enough," remarked the officer. "Still—" He paused as if listening. The noise he heard was Jane Ryder coming from above. He met her half-way up the stairs. "My dear old sis!" he exclaimed as he clasped her in his arms. She said nothing, but sobbed on his shoulder in a hysterical way that was a surprise to me. "Brace up, dear girl," he said, trying to soothe her.

"They were always like that," said the mother in her placid way. "I think it is so nice for brother and sister to be fond of each other. Don't forget that she gave you fair warning." Her attitude and the tone of her voice were so out of tune with all my thoughts and surroundings that I regarded her with amazement. She paid no attention to the look, however, but folded her hands across her ample bosom and smiled at her children in a motherly way.

These children, I knew, were speaking of me, though I could not hear all they said, for the officer—he was Colonel Ryder—laughed and said, "Oh, he'll be in good company. I picked up another fellow in the woods. He says his name is Jasper Goodrum." Then she said something in a low tone, something that caused her brother to regard me with considerable interest.

"Is that so?" he exclaimed. "You must tell me the particulars later; I have no time to hear them now. We must get away from here."

XII

As he said, so it was; he hustled everything before him, permitting me to keep my horse and allowing Whistling Jim to go along. "Good-by, mother," he said; "I'm sorry to leave you in such a place as this. I suppose you are waiting for Major Whiskers." He laughed gayly as he said this, and his mother slapped him playfully as she kissed him.

He invited me to ride with him at the head of his little squad of troops, saying that when a colonel started out to command a corporal's guard he assuredly needed assistance. He was perhaps thirty years old, but he had a tremendous fund of animal spirits, so that he had all the ways of a gay youth of twenty. He paid no more attention to the man who had been knocked about by Whistling Jim than if he had been a log of wood, and yet he was very tendei-hearted. Whatever was in the line of war appealed to his professional instincts. War was his trade, and he seemed to love it; and he had a great relish for the bustle and stir that are incident thereto.

His sister rode in the top-buggy in which I had first seen her, and she might have been the commander of the men, judging from the way she gave instructions. She seemed to know all the roads, for she went ahead without the slightest hesitation. She was driving a good horse, too; his trot was sufficient to keep our horses in a canter; and whenever he heard us coming up behind him he would whisk the buggy away as if he scorned company. Perhaps this was due to the little lady who was driving him.

I had no grudge against her, heaven knows, but somehow I resented my present plight, for which I thought she was responsible. She had given me fair warning, but she should have known that it was my purpose to carry out the orders of General Forrest; and if I was to be warned at all she should have told me the precise nature of the danger. In that case, I could not only have escaped, but I could have been instrumental in the capture of her brother and his whole party. Perhaps she knew this—and perhaps this was why she would give me no definite information.

But if she knew at all she must have known

everything; her brother must have come in response to a summons from her or her mother. In any case I had been tricked—I had been made a fool of—and after what I had done for her, I felt that I had a right to feel aggrieved. Colonel Ryder observed my sullenness and commented on it.

"Don't be down-hearted, my boy. It is the fortune of war; there is no telling when it may turn its sunny side to you. In your place I should whistle and sing and make the best of it. Still, I know how you feel, and I sympathize with you."

"I should not have gone to that house last night," he went on, "but I knew that my mother was there, and I had received information that one of our scouts by the name of Leroy was in great danger of capture. What I did discover was that Miss Ryder had been captured." He laughed as he said this, and gave me a peculiar look.

"As to Leroy," I asked, "was he at that house? I am very much interested in knowing, for General Forrest detailed me to capture him."

"Under the circumstances, you acquitted yourself wonderfully well, and General Forrest has no right to be displeased with you," remarked Colonel Ryder.

"But you have not answered my question," I said.

"In the nature of things," he replied, enigmatically, "I prefer not to tell you. Of one thing you may be sure—Leroy is not likely to bother the rebels for some time to come. I think you have put him out of business, as the boys say."

"Then Leroy must be the name of the man that tried to capture me at the tavern. It was the negro that put him out of business."

"But Leroy is a very dear friend of mine," laughed the Colonel, "and you may be sure I should not have left him there. You observed, of course, that I was very attentive to the man your negro had whipped." He was still laughing, and I could not imagine for the life of me why he was tickled.

XIII

We rode along without adventure of any kind, though I momentarily expected to hear the tramp of Forrest's outriders behind us. They never came, and about ten o'clock—my stomach was my clock in this instance, for I had had no breakfast—we suddenly turned off from the main road and plunged into the shadows of the finest wood I had ever seen. There were giant chestnuts, giant poplars, giant oaks, and giant pines. They were so large that human beings seemed small and insignificant beside them, and I realized that we were in the primeval forest.

The thought, however, did not satisfy my hunger, and I wondered when and where a halt was to be called and rations parcelled out. It is a vexatious feeling for the young to feel the pangs of hunger, and I was not used to a long fast. My feelings were relieved by Whistling Jim, who informed me that he had placed a very substantial ration in my holsters; and I am free to say that, after Colonel Ryder, the negro was the most thoughtful and considerate person I have ever seen. He had an easy explanation for it, and spoke of it very lightly, remarking that all he had to do was to think of himself first "an' de white folks nex'."

In turning into the wood, we were following the lead of the little lady in the top-buggy, and I think that Colonel Ryder had no idea whither she was leading him. Yet he yielded himself and his men to her guidance with a confidence that few soldiers would have displayed. We had come very rapidly until we turned out of the main road, and then we went along more leisurely. This gave me time to overcome my natural stupidity, for I finally realized that our rapid movements on the main road were intended to place us beyond the reach of Forrest's advance guard.

The by-way that we were now following appeared to be little used, yet it was a wide road and a good one, and probably served as the means of communication between isolated farms, or it may have led to some lonely grist-mill which had been built for the convenience of that thinly populated region. Though it was but little used, it was plain to the eye, and I thought with a smile that if Captain Bill Forrest's company should happen to have any leisure a dozen or more of them would be sure to see where it led, in which event——

The smile faded away as soon it came, for I thought of the little lady in the top-buggy who was driving ahead with so much confidence. She would be safe in any event, but what would she think of me if her brother should be captured or killed? I shrunk from facing such a contingency; I shrunk without knowing why. Being a young fellow, and feeling my importance as I have never felt it since, I imagined she would hold me responsible. I had interfered with her plans in more ways than one, and I felt that she owed me a grudge that would grow to enormous proportions should any harm come to her brother.

I was suddenly recalled to the affairs of the moment by hearing the screams of a woman, followed by a rifle-shot. I saw Jane Ryder urging her horse forward, and, without waiting to see what Colonel Ryder proposed to do, I put spurs to my horse, followed by Whistling Jim. The scream of the woman had sent a cold chill all through me, and I was in no humor for waiting to see what the others would do. I thought I heard shouts behind me, but I paid no attention to them. I turned my horse to the left and headed him in the direction from which the sounds had come.

Keeping a sharp eye ahead, I soon came in sight of a cabin sitting lonely and forlorn in the middle of a small clearing. I saw more than this, for three men were engaged in a desperate effort to batter down the door. My horse bore me past the little lady in a flash, although she was using the whip. With a cry of "Halt and surrender!" I rode at the men pistol in hand. They whipped around the house without turning their heads, and ran off into the thick undergrowth, where it would have been both useless and dangerous to pursue them.

They left one of their number on the ground, the victim of the rifle-shot we had heard. He begged lustily for both mercy and water. If he had been compelled to choose between the two I

think he would have taken water. I gave him
my canteen, which he emptied at a gulp and
called for more. There was a strange silence in
the house—a silence in decided contrast to the
screams I had heard, and I wondered if the
wretches had shot the woman. I started to
knock on the door with the butt of my pistol, but
Jane Ryder was before me.

"Only children do such foolish things," she exclaimed, and I thought she had scorn in her voice.
"Sally! Sally Rodgers! Open the door if you
are alive! Don't you know me? Your friends
are here."

"Pardon me!" I said, pushing past Jane Ryder
as the door opened. For a moment I could see
nothing whatever, not even the woman who had
opened the door, but when my eyes grew accus-
tomed to the gloom that pervaded the house—all
the windows were closed—I saw the big Irishman whom I had met at the tavern a few nights
before. He was sitting very quietly in the
chimney-corner, but I observed that he had me
covered with his rifle. I stared at him without
a word, and he was equally as silent, but something in the situation—or in his face, for he had

He had me covered

as pleasing a countenance as I have ever seen—caused me to laugh.

" 'Tis a long mile from a joke," he declared. "Ye see before ye Private O'Halloran av the sharpshooters. Wan av us is a prisoner, an' I'm thinkin' it's not meself."

"It is not given to every man," I replied, "to be taken prisoner while he is still a prisoner. You will have to speak to Colonel Ryder."

The woman had come from behind the door to greet Jane Ryder, and now she was giving her all the details of her troubles, her voice pitched in a very high key. Meanwhile, half a dozen children in various stages of undress swarmed from under the bed and stood staring at us. "The sound of the woman's screams," said I, turning to Jane Ryder, "caused me to forget that I am a prisoner. I hope your brother doesn't think that I made that an excuse for running away."

"And why shouldn't a prisoner escape—if he can?" she asked, after a moment's hesitation. "You'll never have a better opportunity to rejoin your command. You are not under parole, and you are under no obligations to my brother. You

have only to mount your horse, beckon to your
negro, and follow the path you will find at the
back of the house. It leads by a grist-mill. A
part of your command has already passed on the
road beyond the mill, but if you will go now you
will fall in with the rear-guard."

"Beggin' pardon," said O'Halloran, taking
off his hat to the lady, "the lad has engagements
wit' me. He's me twenty-ninth, all told, an'
there's luck in odd numbers. If it's all the same
to you, mum, he'll stay here."

"But it's not all the same to me, Mr. O'Halloran," she said, turning to the Irishman. "I
prefer that he should go."

His eyes grew bigger as he stared at the lady.
"Oh—" he exclaimed, and then paused with his
mouth open. "Niver did I hope to see me gal-
lant Captain in this rig. It doesn't become ye
at all. The trimmin's make ye a fut shorter, an'
be me soul! ye was short enough to begin wit'."
His amazement made her laugh, but she made no
reply.

"Are you going?" she inquired, turning to me.
I hesitated. Undoubtedly here was an opportunity, but something or other—some feeling or

sentiment—call it what you will—held me back.

"Not now," I said, finally. "Some other time, perhaps, but not now." I did not realize at the time why I held back — why I refused to be free."

She turned away from me with a petulant shrug of the shoulders, as much as to say that she was no longer under obligations to me for preventing her capture by the party that had raided the tavern. The big Irishman, who had evidently recognized the little lady as a person of some importance, went so far as to try to persuade me to make my escape, or, rather, to take advantage of the escape I had already made.

"If ye're stayin' thinkin' he's a woman, don't do ut. Don't stop for to say good-by, but straddle yure horse an' be off wit' ye."

But the little lady had a mind of her own, as I was shortly to discover. After she had talked with the woman for a few minutes, she turned to me.

"Will you ride with me a few miles?" she inquired. "Your negro can lead your horse."

I agreed with such promptness and eagerness that a faint tinge of color came into her face.

But, in the bustle of getting away, I paid little attention to her appearance until we were on the move again, and then I observed that she was very pale. I thought it was cold, and said so.

"The wind is certainly chilly," she replied, and then, moved by embarrassment, or stirred by the motherly instinct that constitutes more than half the charm of womanhood, she leaned over and tucked the lap-robe about my knees, and then fell back in her place, laughing gleefully, as a child might have laughed. Indeed, for a woman grown, this little lady had more of the cunning tricks of childhood than anyone I had ever seen— the cute little ways that endear children to those who love them. At the time, this fact did not add to my happiness, for, what with her woman-liness and her childishness, she presented a problem that puzzled and dazzled me, for my mind was wofully lacking in the nimbleness necessary to follow the swift changes of her moods.

She had turned the buggy into the woods, and was driving along with no road to guide her. I had not the remotest idea whither she was carry-ing me, but by way of saying something I protested against the way she was pushing her horse. "You will need him after to-day," I explained.

"I have reason to be in a hurry," she said. "Horses are cheap enough with us. They are furnished by the Government."

"Still, he is a fairly good horse," I remarked, "and he deserves some consideration on his own account."

"Do you think so?" she cried. "I am sure you are very kind—to horses. If I am driving him too hard you have yourself to thank. You have upset all my plans, and I am not very happy. Don't you think a woman deserves as much consideration as a horse?"

"They are to be treated according to their deserts," I answered, gravely. "They know what duty is. Private O'Halloran says that you are no woman, and I say that you are no man. Where does consideration fall in your case?"

"I ask for no more consideration than you would accord to a human being. Mr. O'Halloran has never seen me in my proper dress before, and he knows only how I appear at night when I am working for the cause of the Union. But who are you that you should judge of the deserts of men and women? You are nothing but a boy, and you'll not be different when you are a man. Instead of marching with your comrades, here you are riding in a buggy with a woman—and for what? In the name of heaven, tell me for what?"

She seemed to be overcome by quite a little flurry of passion, and her manner irritated me. "You know why as well as I do," I replied, soberly enough. "You heard the orders my General gave me in the first place, and, in the second place, you know that I am a prisoner. It is odd that you can play a game and forget the score. I imagined when I started that my duty would be the greatest pleasure of my life."

"Do you know where you are going now?" she inquired, very seriously.

"It is a matter of indifference to me," I answered. "Wherever I go, I am in the hands of Providence."

"If you could believe that," she remarked, "it would do you a world of good."

I laughed at her serious manner. "Believe it!" I exclaimed. "Why, it is too plain for mere belief. I do not believe it—I know it."

She was silent for a long time, and when she did speak her words showed that the matter was still on her mind. "It seems to me very peculiar," she said, "that one so young should have such solemn thoughts."

"Why do you call them solemn thoughts?" I asked. "Can anything be more cheerful than to know that you are altogether in the hands of a higher Power—to know that you will be taken care of; or, if you perish, to know that it will be in the very nick of time?"

"You are too serious to be romantic," she said. "I should like to see you making love."

"I can gratify your humor with a right good will—only the lady I would make love to despises me."

"I'll never believe it," she declared, and it was evident that she meant what she said.

"That is because you have only a vague idea of the cruelty of woman when she has a man at her mercy—and knows it."

"I should like to see some woman at your mercy," she said. "No doubt you would give free play to the strap and the rawhide and other implements of the slave-driver."

Her words made me wince, and I must have shown the wound, for when I looked at her her countenance wore an expression of regret and repentance. "You must forgive me," she declared. "If we were to be thrown together you would have to forgive me fifty times a day."

"Well, I thank heaven," I exclaimed, with some feeling, "that I was never at the mercy of more than one woman, and that fact was mitigated somewhat. She was arrayed in the garb of a man, and I was so sorry for her that I forgot she had me at her mercy."

"You should have told her," the little lady declared. "Perhaps if she had known her conduct would have been vastly different. You never know what a woman will do until she has been put to the test."

"She did a good deal," I said, sullenly. "She called me a coward, a rebel, and a traitor."

"Then she must have been in despair," replied the little lady in the most matter-of-fact way. "When you are a little older you will discover that despair has an anger all its own. But I hope you will never feel it," she sighed. "Anyone can see that you know very little about women."

"I hope my ignorance does me no harm," I suggested.

"Not the slightest," she answered. "It is a help to you. It is the sort that goes with youth, and I had rather have your youth than all the experience in the world."

The answer I made I shall always regard as an inspiration. "You can have my youth," I said, "if you will take all that goes with it." For one or two little moments she either doubted her ears or failed to catch my meaning. But when she could no longer doubt—when she was obliged to understand me—she hid her face in her hands to conceal the result of her emotions. I seized her hands and compelled her to look at me. She was blushing like a school-girl. "Is my youth, with all its appurtenances, worth your acceptance?" I asked. She made no reply, and I think she would have maintained silence the rest of the way but for my persistent chattering.

To me her embarrassment was very beautiful —thrilling, indeed—and in some mysterious way her youth came back to her, and she seemed to be no more than sixteen. "My youth is not too youthful for you," I insisted. "I have grown very much older lately, and you have become a girl again in the last five minutes." She was still silent, and I took advantage of it to draw her hands under the lap-robe. "There is no reason why your fingers should freeze," I said.

"They are not likely to—now," she declared, and, though it may have been pure imagination, I thought she leaned a little nearer, and the bare idea of such graciousness on her part seemed to change my whole nature. All the folly of youth went out of me, and love came in and took its place and filled my whole being. What I had been belonged to the remote past; I knew that I should never be the same again.

"I offered you my youth," I said, "and now I offer you my manhood, such as it is. You must answer yea or nay."

She gave me a quick, inquiring glance, and her face told me all that I desired to know. "Neither yea nor nay," she replied. "We are both very foolish, but, of the two, I am the more foolish. We are trying to look too far ahead; we are prying into the future, and the future is away beyond us. Everything you say and everything I have in my mind is absurd, no matter how agreeable it may be. Do you care enough for me to desert your comrades and fling your principles to the four winds? Do I care enough for you to leave my people and give my sympathies to your side?" She was smiling as she spoke, but I knew that she was very serious, and I made no reply. "I am going to tell you the simple truth," she went on. "I do care enough for you to leave everything for your sake, for there can be no real love where there is not a willingness to sacrifice all— Oh, I don't know why women are compelled to make all the sacrifices."

"She not only does that," I replied, "but she is compelled to bear the burden of them alone. Ordinarily, man is a hindrance rather than a help, but I am here to help you."

"Then help me in the right way," she implored.

"I will," I replied; "but here is an argument that is worth all the rest," and with that I drew her to me and pressed my lips to hers. She made no resistance whatever, but somehow the argument did not appeal to her reason.

"I could kiss you twice ten thousand times," she declared, "but facts would remain the same.

I have heard that your people have great notions of honor, and I hope it is true in your case."

Well, it was only too true, and I knew it, but, manlike, I must take some reprisal from the truth. "Your mother told me," I said, "that you have a great knack of hurting those you love."

She leaned against me with a sigh. "If I thought that the truth could really hurt you," she declared, "I should never be happy again in this world, but it is something else that hurts, and it is hurting me a great deal worse than it is hurting you."

I suppose I am not the only man in the world that has been caught in the desert that sometimes stretches its barren wastes between love and duty. I knew that if I but held out my hand to this little woman she would give up all, and, assuredly, had she held out her hand to me I should have flung duty to the winds. But she was of a different mould. The only comfort I had at the moment was in feeling that the sacrifice was mutual.

I longed for her brother to ride up behind us, so that I might still be a prisoner, but she had provided against that. I realized at last that I had never been regarded as a prisoner. I should have been grateful, but I was not—at least, not at the moment. If, as has been said, a man cuts a ridiculous figure when he is sulking, my appearance must have been truly laughable. But the little lady was very sweet and patient. Her eyes were so full of tears, as she afterward confessed, that she could hardly see to guide her horse.

When I came to take note of my surroundings I could not refrain from uttering an exclamation of surprise. We had issued from the forest, when or how I knew not, and were now ascending a very steep hill. Looking back, I saw a mill behind me, and noticed that Whistling Jim was engaged in conversation with the miller. He was evidently negotiating for meal or flour; but it all came to me as in a dream.

"Did you see the mill as we came by?" I asked.

"Certainly," the little lady replied. "Didn't you hear me speak to the miller?"

"I don't know how I am to forgive you for seeing and hearing things. I didn't know we had come out of the wood."

She laughed merrily and laid her face against my arm, but when she lifted it she was crying. "Oh, don't make it too hard for me," she pleaded. "I am not myself to-day. Duty has been poisoned for me, and I shall be wretched until this war is over. Surely it can't last long."

"Not longer than a century," I replied, bitterly.

"Look yonder!" she exclaimed.

We had now reached the top of the hill, and when I looked in the direction in which she pointed, I saw a sight that thrilled me.

XIV

From the crest of the hill a vast panorama, bare but beautiful, stretched out before us.   The hill was not a mountain—indeed, from the direction of our approach, it seemed to be rather an insignificant hill; but on the farther side the land fell away from it quite unexpectedly, so that what seemed to be a hill from one side developed the importance almost of a mountain on the other side.   The road dropped into a valley that ran away from the hill and spread out for miles and miles until it faded against the horizon and was lost in the distance.   The season was winter, and the view was a sombre one, but its extent gave it a distinction all its own.   Far to the left a double worm-fence ran, and we knew that a road lay between, for along its lazy length a troop of cavalry trailed along.

I knew it instantly for the rear-guard of my command, and the sight of it thrilled me.   I suppose something of a glow must have come into my face, for the little woman at my side stirred impatiently. "That is your command," she said, "and you are glad to see them." She was silent a moment, and then, as if she had suddenly lost all control of herself, cried out, "Oh, what shall I do now?"

"You knew what my duty was," I said, with a sustaining arm about her, "and you brought me here."

"But if I had it to do over again I couldn't— I couldn't!" she wailed.

"If you had it to do over again you shouldn't," I answered; and then I seized her and held her tight in my arms. Nor did I release her until Whistling Jim, coming up and realizing the situation, celebrated it by whistling a jig. "If you'll say the word," I declared, "I'll go with you."

"I can't! I can't!" she cried. "Do you say it, and I'll go with you."

But neither of us said it; something beyond ourselves held us back. I am not sure, after all, that it was a sense of duty; but, whatever it was, it was effectual.

"I am afraid something dreadful will happen

to you," she declared. "I have dreamed and dreamed about it. You have made a coward of me. I'm not afraid for myself, but for you."

"One year after the war is over," I said, "I shall be at the old tavern in Murfreesborough. One year to a day. Will you meet me there?"

"I'll be there," she replied, "or send a messenger to tell you that I am dead."

And so we parted. I mounted my horse, and she turned her buggy around. I watched her until she passed out of sight, and I knew that one of her little hands must be cold, for she waved it constantly until a turn in the road hid her from view. On the road toward which she was going I could see a group of men and horses, and I knew that her brother awaited her. With a heavy heart, I turned my horse's head, and went galloping after my comrades, followed by Whistling Jim.

I had but one thought, and that was to report to General Forrest as promptly as possible and receive the reprimand that I knew I deserved. At that time it was the general opinion, even among those of his command who were not thrown into daily contact with him, that this

truly great man was of a grim and saturnine dis-
position. But it was an opinion that did him
great injustice. There were times when he
fairly bubbled over with boyish humor, and
though these moments were rare, he was unfail-
ingly cordial to those that had met his expecta-
tions or who had his confidence. He could be
grim enough when circumstances demanded a
display of temper, but he had never made me
the victim of his displeasure.

I looked forward with no little concern to our
next meeting, for I felt that I merited a reprimand, and I knew how severe he could be on
such occasions. He was far to the front, as I
knew he would be. "Hello, Shannon!" he exclaimed, in response to my salute. His countenance was serious enough, but there was a
humorous twinkle in his eye. "Did you fetch
me the fellow I sent you for?"

Thereupon, I related my adventures as briefly
as I could. He seemed to be amused at something or other—I have thought since that it
must have been at my attitude of self-deprecia-
tion—and called two or three of his favorite
officers so that they might enjoy it with him.

He was highly tickled by the narrative of my experience with the little lady in the top-buggy, though, as a matter of course, I suppressed some of the details.

"Now, I want you all to look at this boy," he said to his officers when I had concluded. "He ain't anything but a boy, and yet he did what no other man in my command could have done. He captured Leroy, the fellow you have been reading about, and fetched him to me, and I've put him out of business. There's Goodrum, an old campaigner, a man who knows every man, woman, and child in this part of Tennessee. I put Goodrum on the same trail, and Goodrum's a prisoner. This boy was a prisoner, too, and yet he turns up all right and puts up a poor mouth about what he failed to do. If every man in my command would fail in the same way I'd have the finest body of troops in the army. And look at him blush. Why, if these other fellows were in your place"—indicating the officers—"they'd be strutting around here like peacocks."

"But, General," I protested, "what I did was through my blundering."

"Then I hope you'll go right ahead with your blunders; you couldn't please me better. I'm going to take you away from the Independents, and I'll put you where I can get my hands on you any hour of the night or day."

And as he said so it was—and so it remained until the close of the war. Especially was it so when Forrest was ordered to cover Hood's retreat after the disastrous affair at Nashville. History has not made very much of this achievement, but I have always thought that it was the most remarkable episode of the war. Under the circumstances, no other leader could have accomplished it. No other man could have imposed his personality between the defeated Confederates and their victorious foe, bent on their total destruction. It was little short of wonderful.

I remember that I was shoeless, along with the greater part of my command, though the weather was bitter cold, and my feet were bleeding, and yet when I heard that trumpet voice, ordering us from the wagons to make one more stand, I never thought of my feet. Nor was there a shirker among the men—and all because the leader was Forrest. Nothing but death would have prevented us from responding to his summons. And we saved that defeated army from annihilation, holding the enemy at bay and driving him back, when, if he had known the true condition of affairs, he would have ridden over us roughshod. There were times when we were upon the point of giving way and fleeing before the numbers that were hurled against us. But always the imposing figure of Forrest appeared at the weak point, and then it would be the enemy would give way.

.   .   .   .

At this point, with only a few more words, my story would have been ended, but the young lady to whom it was first told would not permit it to end there. Her Boston education had not eliminated her curiosity. She sat looking at her mother with an indescribable expression on her face. I knew not whether she was on the point of laughing or crying, and I think that for a moment the mother was as doubtful as I. She did neither the one nor the other, but went to her mother's chair and kneeled on the floor beside her.

"Hasn't Dad left something out?"

"Why, I think not," replied the mother. "Indeed, I think he has told too much."

"Oh, no, not too much," replied the young woman. "I know he has left out something, and I think it is the most important part."

"What I have not told," I remarked, "has been strongly intimated. It is best to leave some things to the imagination."

"I think not," replied the young woman, with decision. "You haven't told anything about what happened after the war."

"That's true," commented the mother, with something like a blush; "but I think that is almost too personal."

"No, no," the girl insisted with a smile; "you know how the public take such things. If Dad writes his story and has it put in a book the readers will think it is pure fiction."

"But if it were fiction," said I, "it would be a bad thing for all of us."

Fiction or not, I was compelled to tell the story until there was no more story to tell.

In the middle of April, one year after the surrender, I made all my preparations to return to

Murfreesborough, and it was no surprise to me that Harry Herndon was keen to go with me. His grandmother made no objection, especially when he explained that he desired to be my best man. His real reason for going, however, was a lively hope that Katherine Bledsoe would accompany Jane Ryder. And then there was Whistling Jim to be taken into account. He made known his intention of accompanying me whether or no. He was free, and he had money of his own, and there was no reason why he shouldn't visit Murfreesborough if he cared to. He settled the matter for himself, and, once on the way, I was very glad to have him along.

But for the subtle changes made by peace, the town was the same, and even the old tavern in the woods had survived all the contingencies of war and stood intact, but tenantless. I made haste to escape from the old house, and was sorry that I had ventured there before the appointed time. The sight of it gave me a feeling of depression, and I had a foretaste of the emptiness there would be in life should Jane Ryder fail to come.

The only consolation I had was in the hopefulness of Whistling Jim. "She'll be dar ez sho' ez de worl'," he said, and his earnestness was so vital that it was the means of lifting me across a very bad place in my experience; yet it did not cure me of the restlessness that had seized me. The night before the appointed day, I wandered far beyond the limit of the town, and presently, without knowing how I got there, I found myself near the house where Jack Bledsoe had lain when he was wounded. I went to the gate and would have gone in on the pretence of inquiring the way to the town; but a woman was standing there in the darkness.

I hesitated, but I should have known her among a thousand—I should have known her if the darkness had been Egyptian. I opened the gate and held her in my arms. Neither said a word, and the silence was unbroken until someone in the house came out upon the veranda and called:

"Jane! Jane! Are you out there? Where are you?" It was the voice of Katherine Bledsoe, and I was glad for Harry's sake.

. . . .

"I don't think that is a very pretty way to

end a story," said the mother of the college graduate, perceiving that I had nothing more to say. "You should by all means get your sweetheart out of your arms."

"Since that day," I replied, "she hasn't been out of them long at a time."

"But you will have to change that part of it when you write the story out."

"Oh, no!" cried the daughter.

I refilled my pipe and listened to their tender arguments until I was sleepy, and when I went to bed they were still arguing.

THE END